Land*Scape*

A YEARBOOK *of*
RECIPES

Published in the United Kingdom in 2015
by Bauer Consumer Media Ltd,
1 Lincoln Court,
Lincoln Road,
Peterborough
PE1 2RF

While all reasonable care is taken to ensure the accuracy of each recipe, the desired results may not
always be achieved due to individual variables such as ingredients, cooking temperatures and equipment
use, or cooking abilities.

Editor: Hilary Scott
Writer: Adèle Donaghie
Art Director: Rachel Hawkins
Home economists: Jacqueline Bellefontaine, Adele Nozedar
Photography: Food & Foto
Illustrations: Shutterstock

Printed by Polestar Bicester
Distribution Frontline (01733 555161)

ISSN 2059-352X

Bauer Consumer Media Limited is a member of the Independent Press Standards Organisation
(www.ipso.co.uk) and endeavours to respond to and resolve your concerns quickly. Our Editorial
Complaints Policy (including full details of how to contact us about editorial complaints and IPSO's
contact details) can be found at www.bauermediacomplaints.co.uk. Our email address for editorial
complaints covered by the Editorial Complaints Policy is complaints@bauermedia.co.uk.

Contents

Foreword

WELCOME TO THE LandScape Yearbook of Recipes. This collection creates a year-round selection of delicious dishes using the best of British seasonal produce. From hearty soups to mouth-watering cakes, it is guaranteed to help you make the most of the fresh ingredients available at every time of the year.

The British Isles has a rich heritage of traditional dishes. For centuries, ingredients for the majority of people would have been limited to what they could forage from hedgerows and woods or grow and farm for themselves.

Out of this need to use local and seasonal ingredients grew a wide range of recipes that were simple to create, but full of flavour. Those in this Yearbook capture the character and flavour of much-loved, tried and tested recipes, passed down through the generations.

Today, top quality British ingredients are easily available. From the milk, free-range eggs, chicken, lamb, beef and pork from our farms to freshly-caught fish, there has never been a time when there has been so much choice. The season's fruit and vegetables, whether from the kitchen garden or greengrocer, bring their different textures, flavours and colour to everyday family meals and special dinners alike.

The recipes in this book are chosen from our favourites published in LandScape magazine. From light lunches to hearty main meals, tempting puddings and melt-in-the mouth cakes, there is something to be enjoyed for every occasion throughout the year.

"And the Spring arose on the garden fair,
Like the Spirit of Love felt everywhere;
And each flower and herb on Earth's dark breast
Rose from the dreams of its wintry rest."

Percy Bysshe Shelley, 'The Sensitive Plant'

SPRING

WITH WARMER temperatures and longer days, this is the season when the land awakens after its winter sleep. Young plants poke through the cold earth in search of the warm rays of spring sunlight. Dishes are flavoured with the first of the fresh herbs, parsley and chives. Wild garlic growing in abundance in woods provides the perfect flavouring for the season's lamb and fish.

It is the time for lighter dishes to grace the table. In particular, fish comes to the fore, whether from the abundant harvest around the coast, or from Britain's rivers and streams. Pots are being readied to catch brown crab, delicious simply dressed or added to soups and salads. Flat fish such as plaice and sole are in season. Pan-fried with butter or rolled in breadcrumbs, their lean, white, meaty flesh responds well to light flavours and cooking. The pink flesh of wild salmon from the rivers and sea is available now, with its lean, salty flavour.

In the garden, brassicas such as cauliflower are burgeoning in the vegetable beds. But king of the spring vegetables is the sweet and nutty Jersey Royal potato. From March, the island's 20 Jersey Royals' farmers are busy harvesting their famous crop, fertilised with Jersey seaweed, known as vraic. High in vitamins B and C, these diminutive tubers are a signature taste of the spring.

In the north of the country, West Yorkshire's famous forced rhubarb is ready to harvest, their stalks a delicate pale pink following a winter spent undercover, starved of sunlight. Cooked in tarts and crumbles, or simply stewed with ginger, it provides a rosy close to a spring meal.

Minted pea and wild garlic soup

Serves 4

small handful of wild garlic, plus extra, chopped, to garnish

350g shelled peas

2 tbsp olive oil

8 spring onions, sliced

225g potatoes, peeled and diced

600ml vegetable or chicken stock

small handful of fresh mint leaves

salt and black pepper

double cream to finish

Heat the oil in a large saucepan and sauté the onions until soft. Add the potatoes and stock and bring to the boil. Reduce the heat and simmer gently for 20 mins. Add the peas.

Roughly chop the wild garlic and mint leaves and add to the pan, simmer for 5 mins. Remove from the heat and allow to cool slightly then purée. Return to the pan and reheat gently.

Season to taste and ladle into bowls. Serve topped with a swirl of double cream and a sprinkle of wild garlic leaves.

Spring salmon flan

Serves 6

For the pastry

250g plain flour

125g cold butter, cubed

2 tbsp chopped fresh soft herbs, such as chives, thyme, parsley, dill or tarragon

2 tsp wholegrain mustard

1 egg, separated

2 tbsp cold water

For the filling

100g asparagus tips

100g small broccoli florets

450g salmon fillets

4 eggs

300ml milk

salt and black pepper

freshly grated nutmeg

Preheat the oven to 200°C/gas mark 6. Sift the flour into a mixing bowl. Add the butter and rub into the flour with your fingertips until the mixture resembles fine breadcrumbs. Stir in the chopped herbs and mustard. Make a well in the centre of the ingredients and add the egg yolk and most of the water. Mix to a dough, adding more water if required. Cover and place in the fridge for 15 mins. Roll out the pastry large enough to line a 25cm deep flan case. Chill for a further 30 mins.

Prick the base of the pastry case all over with a fork and line with a sheet of non-stick baking parchment. Fill with baking beans and bake for 10 mins, remove the paper and beans and bake for a further 10 mins. Brush the inside surface of the pastry case with a little beaten egg white when it comes out of the oven. Reduce the oven temperature to 180°C/gas mark 4.

Meanwhile, blanch the asparagus and broccoli florets in boiling water for 3 mins, then refresh under cold water. Cut the salmon into strips. Arrange the vegetables and salmon in the base of the pastry case. Beat the eggs together with a fork then beat in the milk. Season with salt, pepper and a little grated nutmeg. Pour into the pastry case, return to the oven and bake for 40 mins until the filling has just set. Serve hot or cold.

Plaice goujons with tartare sauce

Serves 4

For the fish

3 plaice fillets

1 tbsp plain flour

salt and black pepper

1 large egg

75g white breadcrumbs

1 tsp dried thyme

sunflower oil for deep frying

For the sauce

½ shallot, finely chopped

100ml mayonnaise

1 tbsp chopped capers

2 tbsp chopped gherkins

2 tbsp chopped fresh parsley

a squeeze of lemon juice,

plus lemon segments to serve

For the fish: skin the plaice fillets and cut in half lengthwise. Slice the fillets diagonally into 1.5 cm-wide strips. Season the flour and toss the fish strips in it to coat.

Whisk the egg and pour into a shallow dish. Mix the breadcrumbs with the thyme and spread out on a plate. Dip the plaice into the egg and then coat in the breadcrumbs. Set the coated fish strips to one side.

For the sauce: place the shallot in a bowl with the mayonnaise, capers, gherkins and parsley. Add the lemon juice and season. Mix well and chill until required.

Heat the oil in a deep frying pan. Fry the goujons in two batches for 3 mins until crisp and golden. Serve immediately with the tartare sauce and a lemon segment.

Devon crab soup

Serves 6

300g cooked white and brown crabmeat

50g unsalted butter

1 large onion

1 stick celery

4 anchovy fillets

500ml whole milk

100g long grain rice

500ml chicken stock

100ml double cream

1 tbsp brandy

salt and pepper

fresh parsley to serve

Peel and finely chop the onion and finely chop the celery. Melt the butter over a gentle heat in a large saucepan. Add the onion and celery and cook, stirring occasionally, for 10 mins until softened. Stir in the anchovy fillets and cook for 2 mins.

Rinse the rice under running water until the water runs clear. Add to the pan with the milk, and bring to the boil. Stir well, then reduce the heat, cover and simmer gently, for 10 mins until the rice is tender. Blitz in a food processor until smooth.

Pour back into the pan and add the chicken stock and crabmeat, stirring well to mix. Bring to the boil gently, then remove from the heat. Stir in the cream and brandy, and season to taste. Serve sprinkled with the chopped parsley.

Watercress potato cakes

Serves 4

40g watercress

400g waxy potatoes

1 small onion, chopped

1 tbsp cold-pressed rapeseed oil, plus extra for oiling

2 tbsp plain flour

2 small eggs

salt and black pepper

Chop the onion, heat the oil in a frying pan and sauté the onion for 5 mins until the onion is softened and beginning to colour. Allow to cool.

Peel and coarsely grate the potato and place in a sieve. Place a saucer or small plate on top and squeeze out as much liquid as possible. Coarsely chop the watercress and add to the grated potatoes along with the sautéed onion. Sprinkle the flour over the mixture then add one of the eggs, beaten. Season and mix well.

Heat a large heavy-based pan and lightly oil the surface. Divide the potato mixture into four and spoon two portions into the pan. Flatten to form a circle approximately 1cm thick. Cook for 4 mins until the underside is golden and crisp. Flip over and cook the other side. Drain on kitchen paper and keep warm while cooking the remaining cakes.

Serve topped with a poached egg.

Savoury cauliflower crustless flan

Serves 8

1 head cauliflower
1 onion
1 red pepper
1 green pepper
1 clove garlic
1 tbsp cold-pressed rapeseed oil
2 tsp fennel seeds
salt and pepper
6 large eggs
125g plain flour
150g Wensleydale cheese
4 tbsp chopped
fresh parsley

Preheat oven to 190°C/gas mark 5. Line the base and sides of a 23cm spring-form tin with parchment paper. Trim the cauliflower and cut into small florets. Steam for 10 mins until just tender. Slice the onion, then deseed and slice the peppers and chop the garlic.

Heat the oil in a large frying pan and sauté the onion and peppers until soft. Add the garlic and fennel seeds, and cook for 1 min while stirring. Whisk the eggs in a large bowl, then gradually whisk in the flour and season well. Crumble in the cheese and add the parsley, sautéed vegetables and cauliflower. Stir gently to mix. Spoon the mixture into the prepared tin and spread level.

Bake for 40 mins until golden and set. Allow to cool for 20 mins before lifting the cake from the tin, taking care to remove any parchment paper, and serve. Can also be eaten at room temperature.

Spinach baked eggs

Serves 4

1 onion
1 garlic clove
1 tbsp butter or margarine
800g fresh leaf spinach
freshly grated nutmeg
8 baguette slices
100g gouda cheese slices
4 sprigs parsley
4 medium eggs
salt and pepper

Preheat the oven to 225°C/gas mark 7. Peel the onion and garlic and chop finely. Melt the butter in a pan. Fry the garlic and onion for 4 mins. Add the spinach and cook covered for 2 mins. Season with salt and nutmeg.

Place the cheese slices on the baguette slices and bake in the oven for 5 mins.

Chop the parsley finely. Divide the spinach among four small, round ovenproof dishes. Crack an egg into each and cook for 10 mins at 150°C/gas mark 2. Season with salt and pepper. Sprinkle the baguettes with pepper and parsley, and serve with the baked eggs.

"I believe in honesty. I believe in a good time. I believe in good food."

Bertrand Russell

Watercress and goat's cheese tarts

Makes 6

500g puff pastry
2 small leeks
25g butter
75g watercress
2 tsp wholegrain mustard
150g soft rind goat's cheese
black pepper
beaten egg, to glaze

Preheat oven to 200°C/gas mark 6. Roll out the pastry to a rectangle a little larger than 24 x 36cm. Trim edges and cut into six equal squares. Lightly score a border around the edge of each pastry square, taking care not to cut all the way through and place on a greased baking sheet. Prick the centre of the pastry with a fork and brush with a little beaten egg. Chill until required.

Slice and wash the leeks. Melt the butter in a small pan and sauté the leeks for 3 mins until softened. Coarsely chop the watercress, reserving a few sprigs for garnish and add to the leeks, then allow to cool. Spread a little mustard over the centre of each pastry square and top with the leek and watercress mixture.

Cut the cheese into 12 slices and place two onto each tart, sprinkled with a little black pepper. Bake near the bottom of the oven for 20 mins until the pastry is risen and golden. Garnish with the reserved sprigs of watercress. Serve hot as a starter or with a salad for a light meal.

Herb crusted lamb cutlets with sautéed leeks and kale

Serves 4

8 lamb cutlets

2 leeks

250g kale

1 red chilli

50g cheddar cheese

50g fresh breadcrumbs

1 tbsp chopped fresh thyme

2 tbsp snipped chives

1 tbsp flour

1 egg, lightly beaten

2 tbsp rapeseed oil

knob of butter

salt and pepper

Trim the fat and meat away from the tip of the bone and lightly season the lamb. Remove the seeds from the chilli, finely chop and place in a mixing bowl. Finely grate the cheese and add to the bowl with the breadcrumbs and herbs, then mix well.

Dust the lamb cutlets or rack with a little flour then dip in the egg and coat in the breadcrumb mixture, pressing the crumbs onto the lamb so it is well covered. Heat the oil in a heavy-based non-stick frying pan and fry the lamb over a medium to low heat for 10-15 mins, turning once.

While the lamb is cooking, slice the leeks and thickly shred the kale. Melt the butter in a pan with 1 tbsp of oil and sauté the leeks for 2-3 mins until tender. Add the kale and a splash of water and continue to cook until the kale is wilted and tender. Season with salt and pepper. Divide the vegetables among four plates, then top the pile with two chops and serve.

Pan-fried slip sole with bacon and cider vinaigrette

Serves 2

2 slip sole, heads removed and cleaned

2 rashers smoked streaky bacon, chopped

3 tbsp cider vinegar

1 large shallot, chopped

3 tbsp cold-pressed rapeseed oil

25g plain flour

salt and black pepper

Heat 1 tbsp of the oil in a large frying pan. Sauté the shallot and bacon until the shallot is tender and the bacon is starting to crisp. Set to one side.

Coat each sole in seasoned flour. Place the remaining oil in the frying pan then add the fish and cook over a moderate heat for 10 mins, turning halfway through.

To test the fish is cooked part the flesh at its thickest point with the tip of a sharp knife. The flesh should look white and come away from the bone easily. Remove the fish and keep warm on serving plates.

Return the shallots, bacon and any juices to the pan. Add the cider vinegar and 1 tbsp cold water and cook while stirring until piping hot. Adjust the seasoning before spooning over the fish to serve.

Sticky treacle-glazed gammon

Serves 6

2kg rolled gammon joint

2 tbsp black treacle

2 tbsp golden syrup

finely grated zest and
juice of 1 orange

2 tbsp wholegrain mustard

Place the gammon in a large saucepan of water. Swirl the pan a few times to rinse the joint, then pour off water and cover the joint with fresh water. Put the lid on the pan, bring slowly to the boil then reduce the heat. Simmer gently for 1 hour 15 mins.

Preheat the oven to 200°C/gas mark 6. Carefully remove the gammon from the pan, placing on a large chopping board. Using a tea towel to protect the hands, carefully cut the strings that tie the gammon and remove the brown skin, leaving as much fat on the joint as possible. Score the fat in a diamond pattern. Line a large roasting pan with a double thickness of foil and sit the gammon in the centre.

Place the treacle, golden syrup, orange zest, juice and mustard in a small pan. Heat gently, stirring until very runny, then brush over the gammon. Roast for 40 mins, basting halfway through the cooking time. Allow to rest for 20 mins before carving.

*"It was wonderful, of course – ham
with mustard is a meal of glory."*

Dodie Smith, *I Capture the Castle*

Milk roast chicken with lemon and thyme

Serves 4

1.5kg oven ready chicken
400ml milk
1 unwaxed lemon
20 sprigs of fresh thyme
salt and black pepper
¼ tsp freshly grated nutmeg
2 tbsp cold-pressed rapeseed oil
8 garlic cloves, peeled

Preheat oven to 190°C/gas mark 5. Season the chicken all over with salt and pepper and sprinkle with nutmeg. Heat the oil in a large frying pan and brown the chicken all over until pale golden. Place in an ovenproof casserole.

If the thyme has woody stems, strip the leaves from the stem and sprinkle over the chicken. If the stems are soft, add the whole sprigs.

Gently crush the garlic with the blade of a knife and add to the dish. Using a lemon zester, remove the zest from the lemon in long thin strips and sprinkle over the chicken. Pour over the milk.

Cover with foil and roast for 1 hour. Remove the foil and continue to roast for 30 mins until the chicken is cooked and the leg bones pull away easily. Remove from the pan and pull the meat off the chicken. Serve with the juices from the dish spooned over the chicken.

Lemon sole with red pepper and herb butter

Serves 4

4 lemon sole fillets
1 red pepper
125g butter
2 tbsp chopped chives
1 tsp parsley leaves
1 tsp thyme leaves
1 leek
1 courgette, plus 1, grated, for serving
salt and black pepper
2 tbsp cold-pressed rapeseed oil

Preheat the oven to 200°C/gas mark 6. Slice the courgettes and the leek. Seed and thickly slice the red pepper.

Place the pepper in a roasting tin and cook in the oven for 15 mins. Allow to cool slightly.

Put the butter, roasted peppers and herbs in a food processor, and season. Blitz until blended. Scoop out the mixture into small bowl, and cover and chill until needed.

Heat the oil in a frying pan and sauté the leeks and courgettes for 5 mins until soft and golden.

Divide among four squares of parchment paper. Place the fish on the vegetables and spoon 2 tbsp of the butter on top of the fish. Fold up the parchment to completely enclose the fish. Place on a baking sheet and bake for 15 mins. Serve the fish in the paper, garnished with grated courgette.

The remaining butter can be stored in the fridge for a week and used to garnish new potatoes, carrots or grilled meat.

Classic roast leg of lamb with Shrewsbury sauce

Serves 8

2.2kg leg of lamb

1 whole garlic bulb, plus 1 extra clove

1 onion

3 sprigs fresh thyme

salt and pepper

2 tbsp flour

450ml red wine

150ml lamb or chicken stock

3 tbsp redcurrant jelly

1 tbsp mild mustard

2 tbsp lemon juice

Preheat the oven to 200°C/gas mark 6. Cut the single garlic clove in half and rub the leg of lamb and the base of an ovenproof dish with the cut ends. Cut the garlic bulb in half. Slice the onion and place in the centre of the roasting dish with the thyme and the two garlic bulb halfs. Place the lamb on top and season. Add 150ml water to the dish.

Roast for 1 hour. Decrease the cooking time by 15 mins for more pink meat, increase by 15 mins for well done. Add a little more water if the dish dries out to prevent the juices from burning.

Remove the lamb from the dish, cover loosely with foil and allow to rest while making the sauce.

Place the dish on the hob and spoon off any excess fat. Over a low heat, add the flour, stirring well to lift up any of the juices from the base of the dish. Gradually stir in the wine and stock. Add the redcurrant jelly and mustard and cook, stirring until the jelly has dissolved. Simmer for 10 mins, stirring occasionally. Stir in half the lemon juice and season to taste, adding a little more juice if required.

Carve the lamb and stir any juices into the sauce before serving the sauce alongside the lamb.

Stuffed chicken with mustard and goat's cheese

Serves 4

4 skinned chicken breasts

150g soft rind English goat's cheese

8 sprigs fresh thyme

1 tbsp wholegrain mustard

8 rashers of smoked streaky bacon

Preheat the oven to 200°C/gas mark 6. Cut a large slit into the long side of each chicken breast and open out.

Cut the goat's cheese into eight slices and place two inside each split. Place a sprig of thyme on top of the cheese. If the thyme is woody, only add the leaves. Close up the breast. Spread a little mustard over the top of the chicken breast, then loosely wrap each stuffed chicken breast with two rashers of bacon.

Place on an oiled baking sheet and roast for 25 mins until cooked through.

Wild salmon and prawn stew

Serves 4

400g wild salmon fillets, skinned

200g cooked peeled prawns

1 onion

1 garlic clove

1 carrot

2 small courgettes

4 tbsp rapeseed oil

2 x 400g can chopped tomatoes

2 tbsp chopped parsley, plus extra
to garnish

300ml vegetable stock

salt and freshly ground black pepper

crusty bread to serve

Peel and chop the onion, crush the garlic. Peel and dice the carrot and courgette.

Heat the oil in a large saucepan and gently sauté all the vegetables for 5 mins until softened. Add the chopped tomatoes, parsley and stock. Bring to the boil, then reduce the heat and simmer for 15 mins.

Add the salmon to the pan in whole fillets – it will break up as it cooks. Cover and simmer for 6 mins, then add the prawns and simmer for another 2 mins.

Season to taste, sprinkle with parsley and serve.

Lamb steaks with savoury rhubarb compote

Serves 4

4 boneless leg steaks or chump chops

3 sticks rhubarb

salt and pepper

15g butter

1 clove garlic, crushed

2 tsp light muscovado sugar

¼ tsp ground ginger

2 tbsp orange juice

¼ tsp dried rosemary

Trim the rhubarb and cut into 4cm lengths. Season the lamb with salt and pepper. Heat a griddle pan over a high heat and when hot add the steaks to the pan and cook for 3-6 mins per side depending on how well the lamb is to be cooked. Place on a warm plate and allow to rest.

Meanwhile, melt the butter in a small frying pan and add the rhubarb. Cook for 2-3 mins until it begins to soften. Add the garlic to the pan, with the sugar, ginger, orange juice and 4 tbsp water. Gently poach the rhubarb for 5 mins.

Serve the lamb steaks with the rhubarb spooned on top and drizzle over the juices. Sprinkle with the rosemary.

This dish goes well with new potatoes and green vegetables.

Rhubarb tart

Serves 8

For the pastry

125g butter, cubed, plus
extra for greasing

250g plain flour

50g sugar

pinch of salt

1 medium egg, beaten

For the filling

500g rhubarb, cut into
15cm lengths

150ml double cream

250ml milk

1 tsp cornflour

½ tsp vanilla extract

2 medium eggs

125g sugar

Preheat the oven to 200°C/gas mark 6. For the pastry: rub together the butter and flour. Add 50g of the sugar, the salt and the beaten egg. Bring the mixture together with a knife to form a dough.

Grease an 20 x 28cm, loose-bottomed tart tin. Roll out the pastry on a lightly floured surface, then line the tin and trim. Chill in the fridge for an hour.

Take the tin out of the fridge. Lay a sheet of baking parchment over the pastry, fill the tin with baking beans and bake for 10 mins. Remove the paper and beans then bake for a further 5 mins at 180°C/gas 4.

For the filling: in a bowl, combine the double cream, milk, cornflour, vanilla extract and the remaining eggs and sugar.

Place the rhubarb pieces in the tin in rows and pour over the mixture. Cook for 35 mins until set. Cool on a wire rack and serve warm, sprinkled with icing sugar.

Chocolate custard eggs

Serves 6

6 eggs
75g milk chocolate
75g plain chocolate (70% cocoa solids)
100ml milk
200ml double cream
25g golden caster sugar
½ tsp vanilla paste
1 tsp cornflour

To prepare the egg shells, gently tap the pointed end of each egg to crack the shell. Carefully peel away the top of the shell wide enough so a teaspoon can be inserted. Using a teacup, gently separate the yolk from the white. Put four of the yolks to one side to use later. Wash the shells in hot soapy water then rinse well. Bring a pan of water to the boil and add the empty shells. Boil gently for 2 mins, drain and allow to cool, then peel away the inner membrane.

Break the chocolate into small pieces and place in a heatproof bowl. Heat the milk and cream together in a small saucepan until just boiling then pour over the chocolate. Stir with a balloon whisk until the chocolate has melted and combined with the milk and cream.

In a separate bowl beat the egg yolks, sugar, cornflour and vanilla paste together. Add three tablespoons of the hot chocolate mixture, stirring constantly. Pour this mixture into the chocolate cream. Place the bowl over a pan of simmering water and cook, stirring until the mixture thickens slightly.

Pour the mixture into a jug, and then pour into the eggshells. Chill for at least two hours before serving.

Blood orange tart

Serves 6

For the pastry

75g butter, softened

50g golden caster sugar

2 medium egg yolks

175g plain flour, plus extra for rolling

For the custard

finely grated zest of 1 orange

400ml milk

3 medium egg yolks

75g golden caster sugar

40g cornflour

4 tbsp double cream

For the oranges

100g golden granulated sugar

2 medium blood oranges

Preheat oven to 190°C/gas mark 5. For the pastry: cream the butter and sugar together until light and creamy. Add the egg yolks one at a time, mixing well between each addition. Beat in the plain flour with a wooden spoon, until the mixture starts to come together. Finish by using the hands to bring the mixture together to form a soft dough. Chill for 30 mins. Roll out the pastry on a lightly floured surface and line a 22cm loose-bottom deep flan tin. Chill for a further 30 mins. Line the pastry case with parchment and fill with baking beans. Bake the pastry blind for 12 mins. Remove the baking beans and parchment, and bake for a further 5 mins. Leave to cool. Reduce the oven temperature to 180°C/gas mark 4.

For the custard: heat the orange zest and the milk in a saucepan over a gentle heat until almost boiling. Remove from the heat. Whisk the sugar and egg yolks together until pale and thick, then whisk in the cornflour. Whisk in a third of the hot milk to the egg and sugar mixture. Mix well, then return to the pan. Cook, stirring continuously until the mixture thickens. Remove from the heat and stir in the double cream. Pour into the baked pastry case and allow to cool.

For the oranges: place the granulated sugar in a wide-based saucepan. Add 100ml cold water and heat, stirring until the sugar has dissolved. Thinly slice the oranges, discarding the first and last slice of each. Add the remaining slices to the pan. Cook at a gentle simmer for 15 mins, turning the slices halfway through. Remove the slices from the syrup. Drain well before placing on a parchment paper-lined baking tray in a single layer. Bake for 20 mins, then leave to cool. Arrange the orange slices over the top of the cooled custard. Chill until ready to serve.

Ginger burnt cream

Serves 4

450ml double cream
6 egg yolks
60g golden icing sugar
2 pieces stem ginger, plus
1 tbsp of syrup from the jar
golden caster sugar

Place the cream in a saucepan and heat gently until almost boiling.

Place the egg yolks in a heatproof bowl with the icing sugar. Beat with a balloon whisk then gradually whisk in the hot cream. Stir in the stem ginger syrup. Place the bowl over a pan of hot water and cook, stirring all the time until the mixture thickens.

Chop the stem ginger finely and divide between four ramekins. Pour over the cream mixture and chill for at least 2 hours.

Sprinkle the caster sugar evenly over the tops and place under a very hot grill to caramelise the sugar. Chill for another hour before serving.

"If more of us valued food and cheer and song above hoarded gold, it would be a merrier world."

J R R Tolkien, *The Hobbit*

Lemon custard pots

Serves 4

4 unwaxed lemons

75g golden granulated sugar

450ml extra thick double cream,
plus extra to serve

5 eggs

1 tsp cornflour

candied lemon peel, to garnish

Preheat the oven to 170°C/gas mark 3. Finely grate the zest from two of the lemons, taking care not to include too much white pith. Squeeze the four lemons until there is 125ml lemon juice. Combine the lemon zest, juice and 25g of the sugar in a small saucepan, and heat gently until the sugar has dissolved. Increase the heat and boil for a few minutes until syrupy. Set aside.

Heat the cream until it just starts to bubble. Place the the egg yolks, remaining sugar and cornflour in a mixing bowl, and beat together until combined. Gradually whisk in the hot cream. Return the cream mixture to the saucepan and cook over a low heat, stirring constantly with a wooden spoon until the mixture thickens enough to coat the back of the spoon. Do not allow the mixture to boil. Remove from the heat and stir in the lemon syrup.

Pour the mixture into four ramekins and place in a roasting tin. Pour boiling water into the tin until it comes halfway up the dishes. Bake for 25 mins until the mixture is set and it wobbles slightly when the dishes are nudged. Remove from the oven and chill the ramekins overnight.

Serve topped with a dollop of the extra thick cream and a slice of candied lemon peel.

St Clement's cake

Serves 8

For the cake

finely grated zest of 1 lemon

3 tbsp lemon juice

150g butter, softened

150g golden caster sugar

3 eggs

200g self-raising flour

For the filling

finely grated zest of ½ orange

2 tbsp orange juice

100g butter, softened

200g golden icing sugar

For the icing

½ orange, zested and juiced

125g golden icing sugar

Preheat the oven to 180°C/gas mark 4.

For the cake: grease and line the bases of two 20cm sandwich tins. Beat together the butter and sugar until pale and fluffy. Add the eggs, one at a time, beating well after each addition. Sift the flour into the bowl before adding the lemon zest and juice. Gently fold into the mixture.

Divide equally between the prepared tins and bake for 25 mins, until springy to the touch. Allow to cool in the tin for 5 mins, then transfer to a wire rack to cool completely.

For the filling: beat the butter until fluffy, then gradually beat in the icing sugar. Beat in the orange zest and juice. Continue beating until the icing is smooth and fluffy. Sandwich the cakes together with it.

For the icing: zest the orange using a zester. Cut zest into very thin strips and blanch in boiling water for 5 mins. This softens it sufficiently to be used as decoration. Drain well. Sift the icing sugar into a mixing bowl and add the orange juice a teaspoon at a time until it is smooth and spreadable. Spread over the top of the cake and sprinkle the orange zest on top. Allow the icing to set before serving.

Chocolate cherry roll

Serves 8

175g plain chocolate
(70% cocoa solids)

400g can cherries

3 tbsp water

4 tbsp brandy

175g golden caster sugar

5 eggs, separated

50g ground almonds

300ml double cream

2 tbsp golden icing sugar,
plus extra to dust

Preheat the oven to 180°C/gas mark 4. Line a 35 x 25cm Swiss roll tin with baking parchment and lightly oil. Break the chocolate into pieces and place in a heatproof bowl with the water and 2 tbsp brandy and stand over a pan of hot water. Do not let the water touch the bottom of the bowl. Allow to stand for a few minutes then stir until smooth and remove from the heat.

Whisk sugar and egg yolks together until very pale, then fold in the melted chocolate followed by the almonds. Whisk the egg whites until standing in stiff peaks. Fold a few spoonfuls of the egg whites into the egg yolk mixture to loosen it, then gently fold in the remaining egg whites. Pour into the prepared tin and spread level. Bake for 15 mins or until springy to the touch. Remove from the oven and cover with a sheet of parchment and a damp tea towel and leave until completely cold.

Drain the juice from the cherries and discard. Place the cherries in a bowl and add the remaining brandy. Leave to marinate while the chocolate roll cools.

Turn out the chocolate roll onto a sheet of baking parchment dusted with icing sugar and carefully peel off the first sheet of lining paper. Whip the cream and icing sugar together until standing on soft peaks. Spread the cream over the chocolate sponge and scatter the marinated cherries on top.

Roll up like a Swiss roll using the parchment to help. Don't worry if it cracks, this is all part of the charm. Carefully transfer to a serving plate and dust with icing sugar. Chill for several hours before serving.

Rhubarb and cinnamon muffins

Makes 12

200g rhubarb, halved lengthways
then chopped
1 tsp ground cinnamon
275g plain flour
3 tsp baking powder
150g sugar
1 medium egg
100ml milk
150ml full-fat yoghurt
80g butter, melted

Preheat the oven to 180°C/gas mark 4.
Line a muffin tray with muffin cases.
Put the flour, baking powder, cinnamon
and sugar in a large bowl.

In another bowl, beat together the egg,
milk, yoghurt and butter, and add to the
flour mixture. Stir, then add the rhubarb.

Divide the mixture between the cases
and bake for 25 mins until firm
to the touch. Serve with a dollop of
whipped cream.

*"Tis an ill cook that cannot
lick his own fingers"*

William Shakespeare, *Romeo and Juliet*

Chocolate truffle cake

For the cake layer

25g cocoa powder, plus extra to dust

50ml boiling water

2 eggs

125g golden caster sugar

100g self-raising flour

2 tbsp rum (optional)

For the truffle layer

300g plain chocolate (70%cocoa solids)

30g liquid glucose

1 tsp vanilla paste

300ml double cream

2 tbsp rum (optional)

flaked sea salt

Preheat the oven 170°C/gas mark 3.

For the cake layer: place the cocoa powder in a small bowl and gradually blend in the boiling water to form a smooth paste. Whisk the eggs and sugar together until very pale and fluffy and the beaters leave a trail when lifted from the mixture. Fold in the cocoa paste. Sift in the flour and fold in.

Pour into a 20cm spring-clip pan and bake for 25 minutes or until springy to the touch. Allow to cool in the pan for a few minutes then transfer to a wire rack to cool complete.

Wash and dry the pan and line the sides with a strip of baking parchment. When the cake is cold place back in the base of the pan. Drizzle 2 tbsp of rum over the sponge if desired.

For the truffle layer: break the chocolate into pieces and place in a heatproof bowl over a pan of hot water. Add the liquid glucose and vanilla paste, and allow to stand for a few minutes then stir until smooth. Remove from the heat.

Whip the cream until just standing in soft peaks, then whisk in 2 tbsp of rum if desired. Fold a few spoonfuls of the whipped cream into the chocolate then fold the chocolate mixture into the remaining cream. Stir until combined. Pour on top of the sponge cake in the pan and chill for several hours.

To serve, carefully remove from the tin and transfer to a serving plate. Scatter with a few crystals of sea salt.

Baked custard cake

Serves 8

125g butter

4 eggs

175g golden caster sugar

1 tsp vanilla paste

125g plain flour

500ml full-fat milk

icing sugar for dusting

Preheat the oven to 170°C/gas mark 3. Melt the butter in a small pan. Generously brush a deep 20 x 26cm ovenproof dish with melted butter then set the rest aside to cool slightly.

Separate the eggs and beat the yolks together with 175g of caster sugar until pale and creamy. Gradually whisk in the melted butter and vanilla paste. Sift the flour over the surface and fold in.

Heat the milk until lukewarm, then gradually stir into the egg yolk mixture until combined. Whisk the egg whites until standing in soft peaks and fold in.

Bake for 30 mins until the top is golden and the custard is just set. Dust with icing sugar and serve.

Hot cross buns

Makes 12

For the dough

500g strong bread flour

2 tsp mixed spice

½ tsp ground nutmeg

7g sachet easy-blend yeast

50g golden caster sugar

1¼ tsp salt

50g butter, cut into small pieces

100g currants

50g chopped mixed peel

1 egg

100ml milk

approximately 150ml warm water

For the cross

60ml plain flour

4 tbsp water

For the glaze

25g golden caster sugar

50ml water

Preheat the oven to 220°C /gas mark 7.

For the dough: sift the flour and spices into a large mixing bowl and stir in the yeast, sugar and salt. Rub in the butter, then stir in the currants and mixed peel. Beat the egg with a fork until broken up and frothy, then beat in the milk. Make a well in the centre and add the milk mixture and most of the water and to mix to a soft dough, adding the remaining water if required.

Turn out the dough and knead well for 5 mins until smooth and elastic. Place in a lightly oiled bowl, turning to coat the dough. Cover and leave in a warm place to rise for 1½ hr until doubled in size.

Turn out onto a lightly floured surface, and lightly knead again. Lightly grease two baking sheets. Divide the dough into 12 and roll each piece into a ball and place on the baking sheet. Cover with a damp tea towel and leave in a warm place until doubled in size.

For the cross: sift the flour into a bowl and stir in enough water to make a soft paste. Spoon the mixture into a disposable piping bag and snip off the end. Pipe a cross on each bun then bake for 15 mins.

For the glaze: place the sugar and water in a small pan and heat gently stirring until the sugar dissolves. Once the buns are cooked transfer to a wire rack placed over a tray or baking sheet and, while they are still hot, brush with the glaze.

The buns are best eaten warm or on the day they are made. They will freeze for up to two months. Defrost in the refrigerator overnight and warm in the oven at 180°C/gas mark 4 for 5 mins.

Almond and coconut tarts

For the pastry

100g sugar

300g flour, plus extra for dusting

1 medium egg

200g butter, cubed

For the filling

20g flaked almonds

100g ground almonds

100g coconut flakes

4 medium eggs

350g butter

150g sugar

1 unwaxed lemon

8 tbsp raspberry jam

icing sugar for dusting

Preheat the oven to 175°C/gas mark 4.

For the pastry: beat 100g sugar, the flour, one egg and the butter until they make a smooth dough. Roll out the pastry on a floured surface, about 3mm thick. Cut out eight circles (14cm) and put them into tartlet tins (11cm). Refrigerate for 30 mins. Prick the tartlet bases with a fork several times and bake for 15 mins.

Separate one egg and beat the egg white. Take the tartlets out of the oven and brush the bases with egg white. Bake the tartlets for a further 2 mins at the same temperature.

For the filling: peel the lemon in fine slivers. Beat 150g butter and 150g sugar together with an electric whisk, until creamy. Add three eggs one by one, as well as the remaining egg yolk, and mix well. Stir in the ground almonds, coconut flakes (leaving a little of both for decoration) and the lemon gratings.

Divide the raspberry jam amongst the tartlets. Divide the nutty paste mix among them and smooth down. Sprinkle the tops with the flaked almonds and coconut.

Bake the tartlets for a further 20 mins. Remove them from the oven and leave in their tins for 15 mins, then take them out and leave to cool. Dust with icing sugar and sprinkle over the remaining coconut.

"The earth had donned her mantle of brightest green; and shed her richest perfumes abroad. It was the prime and vigour of the year; all things were glad and flourishing."

Charles Dickens, *Oliver Twist*

SUMMER

FROM COTTAGE GARDENS to hedgerows, the acid greens of spring have given way to the deep rich hues of summer. Bright flowers nod their heads as busy insects collect food and pollinate the plants, leaving setting fruits in their wake.

Cherry trees have swapped their spring blossom for a covering of fruit. Sweet cherries are best eaten fresh, the sour ones ideal for tasty tarts. In the main paler cherries are sweeter, dark ones are more acidic. Other fruits synonymous with sunny days are fresh raspberries and strawberries. Both are best eaten as soon as possible after picking, bringing the taste of summer to puddings and bakes.

Peas, broad beans and young spinach all deliver the fresh taste of this season, with asparagus the highlight. The slender stems contain high levels of vitamins A and C, potassium, iron and calcium. Delicious lightly steamed, they combine well with bacon or in a quiche.

While asparagus can be enjoyed with minimum fuss, artichokes take a little more time to prepare, but are worth the effort. Pulling away leaf after fibrous leaf from this thistle-derived plant reveals the pale and creamy heart that has a delicate nutty flavour.

Fish remains a staple of the summer menu with both trout and mackerel in season. Steamed, pan-fried or roasted, trout makes a speedy supper. Mackerel's meaty flesh lends itself to rich pâtés and fishcakes. Both are highly nutritious as well as filled with flavour – perfect for summer meals.

Mackerel and crushed potato fish cakes

Serves 4

400g mackerel fillets
750g baby new potatoes,
250ml milk
2 bay leaves
½ tsp black peppercorns
8 spring onions
1 tbsp capers
1 small egg
2 tbsp rapeseed oil for frying
15g plain flour

Scrub the potatoes and place in a saucepan of lightly salted boiling water. Cook for 15 mins until tender. Drain well, then roughly crush with a fork. Leave to cool.

Poach the mackerel, bay leaves and peppercorns in the milk over a low heat for 4 mins. Remove the pan from the heat. Leave the fish to cook in the hot milk for a few mins more until the flesh flakes easily. Drain, discarding the milk and herbs. Flake the fish into large pieces, discarding the skin and any bones.

Trim and slice the spring onions, rinse the capers and roughly chop. Mix the cooled potato, onions and capers with the mackerel then mix in the egg. Form the mixture into eight patties. Cover and chill for a minimum of 30 mins.

Heat the oil in a large heavy-based frying pan over a medium heat. Dust the fish cakes in a little flour. Fry for 5 mins on each side until golden and heated through. Serve with lemon wedges and soured cream.

Asparagus and spicy sausage tart

Serves 8

For the pastry

200g plain flour

100g butter, cold and cubed

50g cheddar, grated

1 egg

pinch salt

For the filling

200g asparagus

100g chorizo, cubed

50g cheese

3 medium eggs

1 tbsp olive oil

150ml whipping cream

sweet paprika

6 sprigs thyme

Preheat the oven to 200°C/gas mark 6.
For the pastry: using a hand mixer, blend the flour, butter, cheese, egg and salt. Briefly knead the mixture into a pastry dough.

Grease an 20cm flan tin with a removable base and dust it with flour. Sprinkle a work surface with flour and roll out the pastry to 30cm in diameter. Line the tin with the pastry, prick it all over with a fork and let it stand for 30 mins.

Bake the pastry blind on the bottom shelf of the oven for approximately 15 mins.

For the filling: fry the chorizo in the oil for 4 mins. Snap off the woody ends of the asparagus, blanche them in boiling salted water for 3 mins, then place into cold water.

Combine the cream and eggs, then stir in the cheese. Add the paprika and most of the thyme, and season.

Pat the asparagus dry and spread over the pastry. Scatter over the chorizo and pour on the cream mixture. Bake on the bottom shelf of the oven for 35 mins. Remove and allow to cool for 5-10 mins before garnishing with the remaining thyme.

Smoked mackerel and cream cheese pâté

Serves 4

280g smoked mackerel fillets

200g full fat cream cheese

finely grated zest of ½ lemon plus lemon juice

2 tbsp chopped flat leaf parsley

sea salt and black pepper

brown bread, to serve

Flake the mackerel into a bowl, discarding the skin and any bones. Mash well with a fork.

Add the cream cheese, lemon zest, parsley, salt and a grind of black pepper. Beat in lemon juice to taste.

Spoon into a dish, cover and chill until required. Serve spread on freshly toasted brown bread.

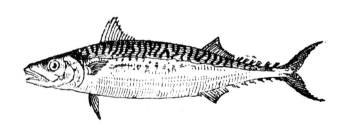

Quail egg salad

Serves 4

12 quail eggs
2 slices of day-old bread
4 rashers of dry cure back bacon
2 cloves of garlic
2 tbsp cold-pressed rapeseed oil
1 head cos or romaine lettuce

For the dressing
1 tsp white wine vinegar
salt and black pepper
150ml cold-pressed rapeseed oil

Bring a pan of water to the boil and add the quail eggs. Return quickly to the boil and cook for 3 mins. Drain and cool the eggs under cold running water. Gently crack, then peel away the shells. Cut the eggs in half and set aside.

Remove the crusts from the bread and discard. Cut the bread into small cubes. Cut the bacon into thin strips and place in a frying pan with the garlic cloves. Cook until crisp, then remove the bacon and place on a plate lined with a sheet of kitchen paper. Add the oil to the pan then toss the bread cubes in it. Cook until crisp and golden. Remove from the pan and add to the bacon. Discard the garlic cloves.

Wash and shake dry the lettuce and cut into bite-size pieces. Arrange the lettuce, bacon, eggs and bread croutons on a serving dish.

To make the dressing, whisk together the ingredients. Drizzle some of the dressing over the salad and serve the remainder on the side.

Devilled lamb's kidneys

Serves 4

4 lamb's kidneys

1 tbsp plain flour

1 tsp cayenne pepper

1 small onion

15g butter

1-2 tbsp rapeseed oil

1 tbsp whole grain mustard

1 tsp Worcestershire sauce

75ml lamb or vegetable stock

4 tbsp double cream

4 slices ciabatta bread

Chopped fresh parsley

Remove the membrane from the outside of each kidney and cut in half. Snip out the core and discard.

Mix together the flour and cayenne pepper and toss the kidneys in the flour mixture. Chop the onion, melt the butter with 1 tbsp of the oil and gently sauté the onion for 2-3min or until beginning to soften.

Add the kidneys and fry for 2-3min each side or until just cooked, then remove from the pan and place on a warm plate to rest. Add any remaining flour to the pan with the mustard, Worcestershire sauce and stock, stir well. Then stir in the double cream and bring to the boil.

Allow the sauce to bubble rapidly for a few minutes until reduced and thickened. Meanwhile, brush the bread with a little oil and toast on a griddle pan until golden.

Reduce the heat, return the kidneys to the pan and gently heat through for about 1min. Spoon onto the toasted bread, sprinkle with some chopped fresh parsley and serve immediately. For a special treat add a splash of sherry in place of the stock.

Courgette and goat's cheese flan

Serves 6

For the pastry

300g flour

2 medium egg yolks

150g soft butter

salt

For the filling

2 courgettes

50g Parmesan cheese

7 stems fresh thyme

200g goat's cheese

1 onion

1 tbsp oil

4 medium eggs

250g whipping cream

salt and pepper

Preheat the oven to 200°C/gas mark 3. For the pastry: put the flour, salt, egg yolks and 3 tbsp water in a bowl. Scatter the chopped up butter on top and work to a smooth dough using the kneading blades of a hand whisk. Wrap the pastry in cling film and leave in a cool place for 30 mins.

Roll out the pastry thinly and line a 26cm flan tin. Trim off the edges. Cover the pastry base with baking parchment and fill with baking beans. Bake the pastry blind for 10 mins. Remove the baking paper and beans and continue to bake for a further 5 mins until golden brown. Remove and turn down the oven to 175°C/gas mark 2.

For the filling: using a fine peeler, remove six long strips from each courgette. Grate the remainder of the courgettes coarsely and put in a sieve. Sprinkle with a pinch of salt and leave to drain. Blanche the courgette strips in boiling salted water for 1 min, drain and spread them out to dry on kitchen towel. Reserve for later.

Grate the Parmesan cheese and pick off the thyme leaves. Divide the goat's cheese roll evenly into 12 slices. Dice the onion finely. Dry off the grated courgette. Heat the oil in a pan and soften the onion. Add the grated courgette and fry for 5 mins. Season with salt and pepper.

Beat the eggs and cream together. Season with salt, pepper and most of the thyme leaves, reserving some for decoration. Tip the grated courgette and onion mixture on to the cooked pastry base. Sprinkle the grated cheese over and cover with the egg and cream mixture. Place the reserved courgette strips on top in a criss-cross pattern and the goat's cheese slices evenly round the edges. Bake until set and the cheese is golden brown.

Chilled tomato soup

Serves 4

1.5kg very ripe tomatoes
3 slices white bread without crusts
1 red onion
1 green pepper
1 red pepper
1 yellow pepper
half a cucumber
2 cloves of garlic
8 tbsp olive oil
3 tbsp red wine vinegar
salt and pepper

Skin the tomatoes by placing in just boiled water for 1 min. Remove with a slotted spoon and dry. Strip off the skin and roughly chop. To remove tomato pips, rub the flesh through a sieve at this point.

Soak two slices of bread in 2 to 3 tbsp of water. Roughly chop the red onion, green, red and yellow peppers, cucumber and garlic. Reserve some of the chopped peppers and cucumber for garnish. Squeeze excess water out of the bread.

Blend the tomatoes, bread, onion, peppers, cucumber and garlic until smooth. Pour in a bowl then mix in 6 tbsp of oil and the wine vinegar. Add salt and pepper to taste. Place in the fridge for at least an hour. Cut the remaining bread into small cubes and fry in 2 tbsp olive oil until browned.

Garnish soup with a sprinkling of chopped vegetables and the bread cubes.

"One cannot think well, love well, sleep well, if one has not dined well."

Virginia Woolf

Lemon and thyme chicken salad

Serves 4

8 sprigs fresh thyme plus extra to garnish
500g chicken breast fillets, skinned and boned
1 small red onion
finely grated zest and juice of 1 lemon
2 tsp whole grain mustard
3 tbsp cold pressed rapeseed oil
100g baby spinach leaves
50g watercress
1 tbsp toasted pumpkin seeds
salt and black pepper

Peel and thinly slice the red onion. Place in a bowl with the lemon zest and mustard, then season with salt and pepper. Strip the leaves from the thyme sprigs and add to the bowl. Toss together well.

Cut the chicken breasts crosswise, into thick strips. Heat 1 tbsp of the oil in a heavy based frying pan then add the chicken. Fry for 8-10 mins, until browned on all sides and cooked through.

While the chicken is cooking, mix the spinach and watercress together. Toss in the red onion slices. Place in a large serving dish.

Once the chicken is cooked, remove from the heat. Transfer to the dish with a draining spoon. Add the remaining oil to the lemon juice and stir well. Drizzle over the chicken and the salad leaves.

Sprinkle the pumpkin seeds over the top of the salad, garnish with thyme and serve immediately.

Baby new potato and beetroot salad

500g baby new potatoes

8 cooked baby beetroot

3 tbsp cold-pressed rapeseed oil

1 tbsp cider vinegar

1 tsp wholegrain mustard

salt and black pepper

8 spring onions, trimmed

2 tsp linseeds

Cut the potatoes in halves or quarters depending on the size. Cook the unpeeled potatoes in lightly salted boiling water for 12 mins until tender when pierced with a skewer. Drain well and place in a serving bowl.

Place the oil, cider vinegar and mustard in a small bowl and season with salt and pepper. Slice the spring onions and add to the bowl. Whisk together until well combined. Pour over the potatoes and toss together so that the potatoes are well coated in the dressing.

Quarter the beetroot and add to the bowl. Toast the linseeds in a dry frying pan over a low heat. Sprinkle over the salad to serve.

Chicken and asparagus pie

Serves 4

500g asparagus

400g chicken breast fillets, cut into pieces

2 tbsp sunflower oil

200g mushrooms, halved

1 onion, chopped

200g carrots, sliced

2 cloves garlic, chopped

2-3 tbsp flour

250ml dry white wine

250ml chicken stock

150ml double cream

1 small bunch parsley, chopped

nutmeg, whole

1 egg yolk

3 tbsp milk

275g ready-made puff pastry, chilled

Preheat the oven to 200°C/gas mark 6. Snap the woody ends off the asparagus and cut it into pieces.

Heat the oil in a large pan. Fry the chicken for 8 mins. After 4 mins, add the mushrooms, onion, carrots and garlic. After 6 mins, add the asparagus. Season. Add the flour, wine and stock, bring to the boil and bubble for 2 mins. Stir in the cream, add the parsley and grate in some nutmeg. Season again.

In a bowl, whisk together the egg yolk and the milk. On a floured surface, roll out the pastry so it is large enough to cover a 20cm wide, 7.5cm deep pie dish. Spoon the filling into the dish and moisten the dish edge with the egg and milk mixture. Place the pastry over the top and press it onto the edge. Trim around the dish. Cut out leaf shapes from the leftover pastry and place on top for decoration. Brush the pastry with the egg and milk mixture. Bake in the oven for 20-30 mins.

Rosemary and bacon wrapped trout

Serves 4

4 trout, gutted and descaled

4 sprigs rosemary

salt and black pepper

1 garlic clove

grated zest ½ lemon plus 2 lemon slices

4 rashers streaky bacon

2 tbsp cold-pressed rapeseed oil

Clean the trout. Season inside and out with salt and pepper.

Strip the leaves from four of the rosemary sprigs and roughly chop. Chop the garlic and mix with the chopped rosemary and lemon zest. Divide into four and place inside each fish. Lay a slice of lemon and a sprig of rosemary on top of each trout. Wrap a rasher of bacon around each to hold the rosemary and lemon in place.

Heat the oil in a large, heavy-based frying pan. Add the trout to the pan and fry for 5-10 mins each side turning occasionally, until the fish is cooked through. Serve immediately.

Pan-roasted artichokes with brown rice

Serves 4

12 prepared artichoke hearts

100g brown rice

1 small onion

1 clove garlic

50g hazelnuts

4 tbsp cold-pressed rapeseed oil

1 tbsp cider vinegar

4 tbsp dry white wine

salt and black pepper

Cook the brown rice in a pan full of lightly salted boiling water for 30 mins, until tender. Drain well and set aside.

Slice the onion and garlic, then coarsely chop the hazelnuts. Heat 1 tbsp of the oil in a heavy-based frying pan. Sauté the onion and chopped hazelnuts for 4 mins until softened. Add the garlic and sauté for 1 min, before adding the artichokes and wine to the pan. Cook for 10 mins, turning the artichokes frequently, until they are soft and the wine has evaporated.

Add the rice to the pan and toss over the heat until piping hot. Mix in the remaining oil and cider vinegar in a bowl, with the salt and pepper. Drizzle into the pan and mix well. Serve immediately or allow to cool and serve cold.

Spicy pan-fried mackerel with coleslaw

For the coleslaw

½ small white cabbage

1 large carrot

1 small onion

5 tbsp mayonnaise

6 tbsp natural yogurt

sea salt and black pepper

For the fish

8 mackerel fillets

½ tsp each coriander, cumin and dried red chilli flakes

¼ tsp caster sugar

2 tbsp plain flour

4 tbsp cold-pressed rapeseed oil

Cut the cabbage into wedges, removing the hard centre core. Finely shred the leaves and place in a mixing bowl.

Coarsely grate the carrot and thinly slice the onion. Add to the bowl, along with the mayonnaise and yogurt. Season and mix well. Set aside while preparing the fish.

Combine the spices, sugar and flour together on a plate, and season. Coat the mackerel fillets with the spice mixture. Heat 2 tbsp of the oil in a large heavy-based frying pan. Fry two fillets for 2 mins each side until golden. Keeping the cooked fillets warm, repeat with the remaining fish, adding more oil if required.

Serve with the coleslaw.

New potato and creamy leek bake

Serves 4

1kg new potatoes, peeled

2 leeks

4 rashers dry cure back bacon

4 eggs

400ml double cream

150ml milk

100g mature Cheddar cheese

20g butter

salt and black pepper

Preheat the oven to 180°C/gas mark 4. Generously grease a shallow ovenproof dish with some of the butter. Cook the unpeeled potatoes in lightly salted boiling water for 10 mins until just tender when pierced with a skewer. Trim and slice the leeks then wash well.

Remove the rind from the bacon and cut into strips. Melt the remaining butter and gently sauté the leeks and bacon for 5 mins.

Place the eggs in a bowl and beat with a fork to break up. Beat in the milk and cream. Season well with salt and pepper.

Thickly slice the potatoes. Spread one third of the potato slices in a layer in a shallow ovenproof dish. Top with half the leek and bacon mixture. Repeat the layers, finishing with a layer of potatoes. Pour the cream mixture over the top. Coarsely grate the cheddar and sprinkle on top.

Bake for 30 mins in the oven until the top is golden and the mixture has set.

Fresh bean salad

Serves 4

250g green beans

300g shelled baby broad beans

1 red onion

4 large tomatoes

For the mint dressing

4 tbsp cold-pressed rapeseed oil

2 tbsp lemon juice

2 tbsp chopped fresh mint

1 tsp light Muscovado sugar

salt and black pepper

Top and tail the green beans. Bring a large pan of water to the boil. Add the beans to the water and bring quickly back to the boil. Simmer for 4-5 mins until just tender. Remove with a draining spoon and place in a bowl of iced water.

Add the shelled broad beans to the water and return to the boil. Reduce the heat and simmer for 5 mins until tender. Drain and add to the iced water. Drain all the beans well and transfer to a serving bowl.

Thinly slice the red onion and add to the beans. Cut the tomatoes in half, scoop out and discard the seeds. Dice the tomato flesh and add to the bowl.

Combine the ingredients for the dressing in a small bowl and whisk well with a fork. Pour over the salad and toss to combine. Chill the salad until required.

Pan-fried sea bass with lemon and wild garlic

Serves 2

2 sea bass fillets

grated zest and juice of ½ lemon

small handful of wild garlic leaves

1 tbsp rapeseed oil

knob of butter

100ml double cream

salt and black pepper

Season the fish fillets with salt and black pepper. Thinly shred the garlic leaves.

Heat the oil in a frying pan and add the butter. When the butter is sizzling, add the fish skin-side up and fry for 1 min. Turn over and cook for a further 3 mins until the fish is cooked through. Remove from the pan and keep warm.

Deglaze the pan with the lemon juice and stir in the lemon zest and double cream. Add the garlic leaves and simmer for 2 mins until the sauce is reduced and thickens slightly.

Serve with the sauce spooned over the top of the fish.

Raspberry summer pudding

Serves 6

500g raspberries

250g redcurrants

3 tbsp golden caster sugar

4 tbsp raspberry flavoured liqueur

6-8 slices day-old bread

Cream to serve

Place raspberries, redcurrants and caster sugar in a pan and cook gently for 15 mins until soft and juicy. Stir in raspberry liqueur.

Remove crusts from the bread. Spoon a little fruit juice into a 900ml pudding basin. Line the base with bread, torn to fit the circle snugly. Spoon in some of the fruit. Continue layering fruit and bread, finishing with a layer of bread.

Place a saucer on top to weight down. Chill for a minimum of 8 hrs. Carefully turn out onto a dish. Serve cut into slices with cream.

Cherry lattice pie

For the pastry

300g plain flour

2 tbsp icing sugar

150g butter

1 egg, separated

4 tbsp cherry jam

For the filling

750g fresh cherries

2 tbsp golden caster sugar, plus extra to sprinkle

1 tbsp cornflour

Preheat the oven to 200°C/gas mark 6.
For the pastry: sieve the flour and icing sugar into a large bowl. Add the butter, cut into cubes, and rub in until the mixture resembles fine breadcrumbs. Add the egg yolk to the bowl with 1-2 tbsp water to mix to a dough. Allow to rest in the refrigerator for 15 mins.

Roll out three-quarters of the pastry on a lightly-floured surface. Use to line the base and sides of a 23cm round pie plate. Spread the jam over the base of the pastry case.

For the filling: Pit the cherries and place in a bowl. Combine the caster sugar and cornflour together and sprinkle over the cherries then toss it all together. Pile the mixture into the pastry case and level out.

Roll out the remaining pastry and cut it into strips. Arrange in a lattice pattern over the cherries. Secure the pastry at the edges with beaten egg white. Brush the top of the pastry with egg white and sprinkle with caster sugar. Chill for 30 mins.

Bake for 20 mins then reduce the oven temperature to 180°C/gas mark 4. Bake for a further 30-40 mins, until the pastry is crisp and golden.

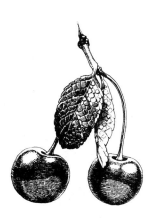

Elderflower and raspberry jellies

Makes 6

8 tbsp elderflower syrup
275g raspberries
570ml cold water
11g powdered gelatine

Dilute 7 tbsp of the elderflower syrup in the water, then spoon 4 tbsp of the dilution into a pan. Sprinkle the gelatine over the top and leave for 15 mins.

Divide the raspberries among six empty jam jars.

Place the pan over a very low heat and stir to dissolve the gelatine. Take care not to bring the solution to the boil or the jelly will not set. Pour the rest of the diluted syrup into the pan and stir well. Pour over the raspberries.

Leave to cool then refrigerate for a minimum of 3 hrs before serving. Drizzle the final tbsp of syrup on top of each jelly before serving.

"The preparation of good food is merely another expression of art, one of the joys of civilised living."

Dione Lucas

Raspberry and coconut ice lollies

Makes 6

200g raspberries

50g golden caster sugar

1 tbsp cornflour

100g icing sugar

400ml coconut milk

50g desiccated coconut

grated zest of 1 lime

Combine the raspberries and caster sugar in a bowl and mash well with a fork, and reserve.

Place the cornflour and icing sugar together in a saucepan and gradually whisk in the coconut milk. Heat gently, stirring constantly until the mixture thickens. Remove from the heat and stir in the desiccated coconut and zest. Allow to cool, stirring from time to time to prevent a skin forming.

Divide the mixture into two halves. Stir a quarter of the reserved crushed raspberries into one half of the mixture.

Divide the raspberry and coconut mixture between six lolly moulds. Add the remaining crushed raspberries to the moulds and then top with the plain coconut mixture. Swirl the raspberries and coconut together a little with a small knife. Insert lolly sticks, then freeze until solid. Turn out of the moulds to serve.

Kentish batter pudding

Serves 4

500g fresh cherries
50g butter, plus extra for greasing
50g plain flour
50g golden caster sugar
2 eggs
300ml milk
icing sugar to dust

Preheat the oven to 220°C/gas mark 7. Generously grease a 1.5 litre shallow ovenproof dish with butter. Pit the cherries and place half of them in the dish. Place in the oven to heat for 5 mins.

Combine the plain flour and caster sugar in a mixing bowl and make a well in the centre. Separate the eggs and add the yolks to the centre of the bowl with 3-4 tbsp milk. Beat until smooth then gradually beat in the remaining milk. Melt the butter and stir in.

Whisk the egg whites until standing in soft peaks and gently fold in with a metal spoon or spatula. Pour the batter over the hot cherries.

Drop the remaining cherries into the batter and return to the oven. Bake for 15 mins. Reduce the heat to 180°C/gas mark 4 and bake for a further 20 mins.

Allow to stand for 10 mins before serving, dusted with icing sugar.

Elderflower and lemon cheesecake

Serves 8

2 tbsp elderflower syrup

zest of 2 lemons

200g plain digestive biscuits

90g unsalted butter

60g golden caster sugar

360g marscapone cheese

160ml double cream

pinch of powdered cardamom

single elderflowers to decorate

Put the biscuits in a bowl and crush with a rolling pin until they resemble breadcrumbs. Melt the butter in a pan and add the crushed biscuits, sugar and cardamom. Mix well so all the dry ingredients are covered with the butter. Press the mixture firmly into the bottom of a 20cm loose-bottomed baking tin. Refrigerate for an hour until set.

Gently stir together the mascarpone, the zest of one of the lemons and the elderflower syrup, then fold in the double cream. Spoon out onto the top of the biscuit base, spreading smoothly over it. Chill in the fridge for 3 hrs.

Prior to serving, sprinkle the surface of the cheesecake with the zest of the second lemon and scatter over the single flowers.

Strawberry pancakes

Makes 10

6 large strawberries
225g plain flour
4 tsp baking powder
1 pinch of salt
2 medium eggs, separated
300ml milk
2 tbsp butter
20g butter
200g Greek-style yogurt
150ml maple syrup

Sieve the flour, baking powder and salt into a bowl and make a hole in the middle. Beat the yolks and add to the hole with a little of the milk. Using a wooden spoon, work the egg/milk mixture in with the flour, gradually adding milk to make a smooth batter. Melt the butter and stir it in. Cool for 15 mins.

Slice the strawberries thinly. Heat a little butter in a frying pan and add a ladle of pancake mixture. Spread out some strawberry slices in a circle on the pancake. When it starts to bubble, turn over and finish cooking for a maximum of 1 min.

Do the same with the remainder of the mixture, keeping the cooked pancakes warm. Arrange the pancakes on plates with yogurt and drizzle with maple syrup.

Butterfly cakes with gooseberry curd

Makes 12

For the curd
500g gooseberries
1 unwaxed lemon
120g butter, softened
120g golden caster sugar
2 eggs

For the cakes
125g butter
300g golden caster sugar
4 large eggs
120g self-raising flour
Icing sugar for sprinkling

Preheat the over to 180°C/gas mark 4.

For the curd: rinse the gooseberries. Grate the zest from the lemon and squeeze the juice. Cut the butter into cubes. Place the gooseberries and 2 tbsp water in a small saucepan and cook gently for 15 mins until they are very soft. Allow to cool, then push through a nylon sieve.

Place the purée in a heatproof bowl, with the lemon zest, juice, butter and sugar. Place over a saucepan of simmering water and cook. Stir constantly until the butter has melted and the sugar dissolved. Whisk the eggs together then strain into the bowl, whisking well. Continue to cook until the mixture is thick and leaves a slight trail when the whisk is lifted up.

For the butterfly cakes: place the sugar and butter in a mixing bowl and cream together until light and fluffy. Beat the eggs in one at a time. Fold in the flour. Line a bun tray with 12 fairy cake cases and divide the cake mixture equally between them. Bake in the oven for 15 to 20 mins until springy to the touch. Transfer the cakes to a wire rack to cool.

Cut a slice from the top of each cake and halve it. Spoon curd into the centre of each cake and place the half slices of cake on top to resemble butterfly wings. Sprinkle with icing sugar to serve. Any leftover curd can be poured into a sterilised jar and stored in a refrigerator for up to one month.

Raspberry tarts

For the pastry

150g plain flour

25g ground almonds

75g butter

50g icing sugar

2 egg yolks

For the filling

300g raspberries

250g crème fraîche

25g icing sugar

grated zest 1 lemon

3 tbsp seedless raspberry jam

Preheat the oven to 200°C/gas mark 6.

For the pastry: place the flour and ground almonds in a mixing bowl. Cut the butter into cubes and rub in until the mixture resembles fine breadcrumbs. Stir in the icing sugar. Add the egg yolks and mix to a soft dough, adding a little cold water if required. Cover and allow the pastry to rest for 15 mins, then divide into 6 equal portions.

Roll each piece into a circle approximately 3mm thick. Press the pastry circles gently into 6 x 12cm individual tart tins. Prick the bases with a fork. Line each case with baking parchment and baking beans. Chill for 15 mins.

Place on a baking sheet and bake in the oven for 10 mins, then remove the paper and beans. Return to the oven and bake for a further 10 mins, until the pastry is crisp and golden. Allow to cool.

For the filling: place the crème fraîche in a bowl and stir in the icing sugar and the lemon zest. Divide the mixture between the cooled pastry cases. Arrange the raspberries on top. Warm the jam in a small saucepan with a little water and spoon over the raspberries to glaze.

Cherry Bakewell

Serves 8

For the pastry

175g plain flour

1 tbsp icing sugar

85g butter

For the filling

250g fresh cherries

125g butter, softened

125g golden caster sugar

2 eggs

150g ground almonds

25g flaked almonds

Preheat the oven to 200°C/gas mark 6.
For the pastry: place the flour and icing sugar into a mixing bowl. Cut the butter into cubes and add to the flour and sugar. Rub the butter into the flour until the mixture resembles fine breadcrumbs. Add enough cold water to mix to a dough and allow to rest for 10 mins. Roll out the pastry and use to line a 20cm round fluted flan case. Chill for 30 mins.

Line the pastry case with baking parchment and fill with baking beans. Bake in the oven for 10 mins. Remove the paper and beans and bake for a further 5-10mins until just golden.

Reduce the oven to 180°C/gas 4.

For the filling: pit the cherries. Beat together the remaining butter and sugar until pale and fluffy. Beat in the eggs one at a time, then fold in the ground almonds.

Place the pitted cherries in the pastry case and spoon over the almond mixture. Spread the mixture so that it covers the cherries. Sprinkle with the flaked almonds. Bake for 35-40 mins until the filling is well risen and golden. Allow the tart to cool for a minimum of 15 mins before removing from the tin. Serve hot or cold.

Elderflower cream tarts

For the pastry cases

200g plain flour

2 tbsp icing sugar, plus extra for dusting

100g cold unsalted butter, diced, plus extra for greasing

1 egg

1 tbsp elderflower syrup

For the filling

125ml elderflower syrup

300ml double cream

30g white caster sugar

juice of 1 lemon

single elderflowers to decorate

Preheat the oven to 150°C/gas mark 2.
For the pastry: sift the flour and the icing sugar into a bowl then rub in the cold butter. Beat the egg and syrup together. Add this to the mixture, a little at a time, mixing to a dough. Knead lightly on a surface dusted with icing sugar. Wrap the dough in cling film and refrigerate for 30 mins.

After the pastry has chilled, roll it out on a surface dusted with icing sugar. Cut 12 x 7.5cm circles. Place a pastry disc into a depression of a greased bun tin, then cover with a circle of baking parchment and a few baking beans. Repeat the process to fill all the depressions. Bake in the oven for 25 mins until golden. Take out, remove the baking beans and paper, and leave to cool.

For the filling: put the cream, syrup and caster sugar into a pan. Bring slowly to boiling point, then turn down the heat. Add the lemon juice and simmer for 3 mins. Scoop the mixture into the tart cases, leave to cool then refrigerate for 4 hrs until set.

Dust the tarts with icing sugar and decorate with a sprinkle of elderflowers.

Carrot, courgette and orange cake

Serves 12

For the cake

150g courgettes

1 pinch salt

100g carrots

2 medium eggs

125ml rapeseed oil

150g sugar

225g plain flour

3 level tsp baking powder

½ tsp bicarbonate of soda

For the filling

75g butter

2 unwaxed oranges

3 medium eggs

75g sugar

For the topping

200g double cream soft cheese

50g icing sugar

Preheat the over to 175°C/gas mark 2.

For the cake: grate the courgettes coarsely. Place in a sieve, sprinkle with a pinch of salt and leave to drain. Peel and coarsely grate the carrots. Grease the bases of 2 spring-form 20cm cake tins and cover with greaseproof paper.

Beat the eggs, oil and 150g sugar with an electric whisk until the mixture is white and fluffy. Mix together the flour, baking powder and bicarbonate. Sieve on to the egg mixture and combine well. Stir in the courgette and carrot gratings.

Divide the mixture between the two cake tins. Bake in the oven for 30 mins, until an inserted skewer comes out clean. Remove from the oven. Leaving in the tins to cool slightly, before removing. Let the cakes cool completely on a wire rack.

For the filling: melt the butter in a pan. Wash the oranges in hot water and pat dry. Peel the skin from 1 orange in thin strips and remove just the zest from the other. Halve the oranges and extract the juice. Reserve 1-2 tbsp of juice and the zest for the topping. Add the eggs, sugar, 125ml orange juice and the peel to the pan. Stir over a low heat to make a thick sauce. Cool.

For the topping: stir the cream cheese until smooth. Sieve the icing sugar over it and mix well. Stir in 1-2 tbsp of orange juice.

Place one cake on a plate, spread with the orange curd and place the second cake on top. Decorate with the cream cheese and orange zest.

"To bend with apples the moss'd cottage-trees,
And fill all fruit with ripeness to the core;
To swell the gourd, and plump the hazel shells
With a sweet kernel"

John Keats, 'Ode to Autumn'

AUTUMN

THIS IS THE SEASON of plenty. After a summer of growth, fruit and veg are ripe and ready to be harvested. A countryside ramble yields a bounty of wild rewards. Hedgerows are a rich source of natural ingredients. The branches of brambles become heavy with luscious blackberries. Rich in vitamin C, these juicy fruits are a seasonal treat, topped with crumble and served with cream. Another wild fruit packed full of goodness is the rosehip. Remaining long after the rose petals have fallen, rosehips can be made into syrups or added to cakes. While nearly all roses produce hips, *Rosa rugosa* are the tastiest having a fruity, spicy flavour.

The midnight blue skins of damsons cover the honey yellow flesh as they weigh down branches of trees along country lanes and riverbanks. The strong, sour flavour of these wild fruits are excellent in jams while adding depth and colour to savoury dishes.

In the vegetable patch, the golden pumpkins brighten beds. Their tough shells are carved for Hallowe'en lamps. The honeyed flesh inside, high in vitamins and fibre, adds sweetness and a velvety texture to warming soups.

A very seasonal ingredient is ripening in the orchards of Kent. Cobnuts, a cultivated form of the hazelnut, are soft and green through the summer, but in autumn the shells harden and the nut inside turns brown. They can be eaten raw but their flavour intensifies when roasted.

Mussels with thyme and bacon

Serves 4

1kg fresh mussels

125g smoked bacon lardons

2 tbsp lemon thyme leaves
plus sprigs to garnish

2 small leeks

1 tbsp cold-pressed rapeseed oil

25g butter

grated zest 1 lemon

250ml dry cider

pepper to season

Scrub the mussels and pull away the beards. Discard any mussels that have broken shells or do not close when tapped.

Trim the leeks and thinly slice, wash well and shake away as much water as possible.

Heat the oil in a large saucepan and add the bacon lardons. Cook until they begin to crisp and brown. Add the butter to the pan. When it has melted, stir in the leeks and lemon thyme. Cook for 5 mins, stirring frequently until the leeks have softened. Turn the heat up high, add the mussels, lemon zest and cider. Cover and cook for 4-5 mins, shaking the pan occasionally, until the mussels have opened.

Remove the mussels, bacon and leeks with a draining spoon and place in a warm serving bowl. Discard any that have not opened.

Boil the juices left in the pan for 2 mins until reduced slightly. Pour over the mussels in the bowl. Season with black pepper, garnish with thyme sprigs and serve.

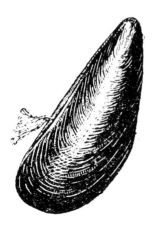

Pumpkin and pear soup

Serves 6

900g pumpkin flesh, cut into chunks

2 pears, peeled, cored and sliced

1 large onion, chopped

1 clove garlic, chopped

40g butter

1 tbsp mild curry powder

600ml vegetable stock

2 to 3 sprigs fresh thyme

2–3 tbsp double cream (optional)

300ml milk

salt and black pepper

50g Stilton cheese

Heat the butter in a large saucepan and sauté the pumpkin chunks, onion and garlic for 10 mins. Add the curry powder then stir in the stock and thyme. Bring to the boil, then cover, reduce the heat and simmer for 30 mins.

Place the pear slices in a small pan with 2 tbsp water. Cover and cook gently for 10 mins until very soft. Purée in a liquidiser or food processor. Stir in the double cream, if using, and set aside.

Remove the thyme sprigs, purée the soup and return to the pan. Add the milk and heat gently. Season to taste with salt and pepper.

Serve the soup with a swirl of pear purée and crumbled Stilton on top.

Creamy garlic and thyme mushrooms

Serves: 4

2 tbsp fresh thyme leaves
250g mushrooms
1 clove garlic
1 tbsp cold-pressed rapeseed oil
25g butter
100ml crème fraîche
salt and pepper
4 slices sour dough bread

Slice the mushrooms and chop the garlic.

Heat the oil and butter in a small frying pan and sauté the mushrooms for a few minutes until beginning to soften. Add the garlic and thyme. Cook until all the mushrooms are tender.

Toast the bread. Add the crème fraîche to the pan and heat through gently.

Season to taste and serve on top of the toasted sour dough.

"No cook who has attained mastery over her craft ever apologises for the presence of garlic in her productions."

Ruth Gottfried, *The Questing Cook*

Chicken liver pâté

Serves 4

300g chicken livers
250g butter
1 small red onion, finely chopped
1 clove garlic, crushed
3 tbsp dry sherry
salt and black pepper
toasted sourdough bread, to serve

Cut the butter into small cubes. Place in a small saucepan over a very low heat until the butter melts and the milk solids separate and sink to the bottom of the pan. Allow the butter to cool slightly, then carefully pour the clarified butter into a jug, discarding the milk solids.

Trim the livers, rinse and pat dry on kitchen paper. Cut each liver into three pieces. Pour 2 tbsp of the clarified butter into a small frying pan and sauté the onion for 3 mins until softened. Add the garlic and cook for 1 min.

Add the chicken livers to the pan. Cook over a medium high heat for 2 mins until they are browned and cooked through. Do not over cook or they become tough. Add the sherry to the pan. Cook for 3 mins to boil off the alcohol and reduce to 1 tbsp. Remove from the heat, season well and place in the bowl of a food processor. Blitz until smooth, add 100ml of the clarified butter and blitz again briefly to combine.

Spoon the pâté into one large or four individual serving dishes and level the top. Pour the remaining clarified butter over the top of the pâté and chill for 2 hrs before serving. Serve with thinly sliced, toasted sourdough bread.

Mulligatawny

Serves 4

1 chicken breast

1 onion

1 carrot

1 small eating apple

25g butter

2 tbsp curry paste

400g tin chopped tomatoes

1 litre chicken or vegetable stock

4 tbsp cooked rice

Finely chop the onion and carrot. Peel, core and dice the apple. Dice the chicken breast.

Melt the butter in a large saucepan and fry the onion and carrot until they begin to soften. Add the chicken and cook for 5 mins. Stir in the curry paste and cook for 2 mins. Add the apple, tomatoes and stock, and bring to the boil. Cover and simmer gently for 25 mins.

Serve with a portion of cooked rice spooned into the centre of the soup.

Chestnut and bacon salad

Serves 6

175g cooked chestnuts

12 thin rashers dry cure streaky bacon

3 slices crusty bread

6 tbsp cold-pressed rapeseed oil

70g rocket

1 carrot

1 green eating apple

1 small red onion

2 tbsp cider vinegar

1 tsp wholegrain mustard

salt and pepper

Preheat the oven to 200°C/gas mark 6. Place the bacon on a baking tray and cook in the oven for 10 mins until crispy. Transfer to a plate and allow to cool. Cut the bread into cubes and scatter onto the tray the bacon was cooked on. Toss in the fat from the bacon. Drizzle with 2 tbsp of oil, then season lightly with salt and pepper. Bake for 12-15 mins until the bread is browned and crisp. Place on kitchen paper and leave to cool.

Meanwhile, put the rocket leaves in a bowl. Add the chestnuts, while breaking them into pieces. Trim the carrot and shave into ribbons with a potato peeler. Add to the bowl with the thinly sliced red onion. Just before serving, core and thinly slice the apple and add to the bowl.

In a small bowl, whisk together the remaining oil, vinegar and mustard with a little seasoning. Pour over the ingredients in the bowl and toss to combine. Add the toasted bread cubes. Divide equally between 6 serving plates. Top each salad with the crispy bacon rashers broken in half. Serve immediately.

Chicken, ham and wild mushroom pie

Serves 6

850g fillets of chicken thighs, each cut into 4 pieces

400g ham, cut into small pieces

200g chunky wild mushrooms

2 tbsp olive oil

2 red onions, peeled and cut into chunks

2 large leeks, peeled and chopped

2 whole cloves garlic, crushed

large knob of butter

75g flour (plain or self raising) plus extra for dusting

350ml stock (chicken or vegetable)

350ml milk

2 tsps dried herbs

300g puff pastry, at room temperature

1 egg, beaten

Preheat the oven to 200°C/gas mark 6. Add the oil to a large pan, and fry the onions and leeks for 10 mins. Towards the end of this time, add the garlic. Remove the vegetables from the pan with a slotted spoon and put in the chicken. Season and fry for 5 mins until golden. Add the mushrooms, cook for another 5 mins, then add the ham. Stir then spoon into a 2.5 litre ovenproof pie dish.

Melt the butter in a second pan. Add the flour gradually, stirring all the time. Pour in the stock with the milk, a little at a time. Bring to a rolling boil for 5 mins. Add the dried herbs. Pour the liquid over the chicken, ham and mushrooms and stir everything together.

Dust a surface with flour and roll out the pastry to the shape of the dish, leaving an inch extra around the edges. Cut a small hole in the centre. Brush egg around the rim of the dish, then top with the pastry. Press down the edges to make a seal. Make decorative shapes from the pastry off-cuts and stick to the lid with water. Brush the pastry with egg. Bake the pie for 30 mins, until the pastry is crisp and golden.

Cinnamon beef casserole

Serves 4

1kg diced stewing beef

2 cinnamon sticks

2 garlic cloves

400ml red wine

6 bay leaves

150g smoked, mature bacon

1 tbsp butter

1 tbsp flour

salt and pepper

6 shallots

500g baby carrots

500g turnips

500g potatoes

100g dried prunes

Wash the meat and pat dry. Peel and crush the garlic. Mix with the wine, meat, cinnamon and bay leaves and leave overnight.

Preheat the oven to 175°C/gas mark 4. Drain the meat into a sieve while saving the marinade. Remove the bay leaves and cinnamon from the meat and put back with the marinade. Dry the meat well.

Cut the bacon into small strips. Heat the butter in a lidded casserole tin. Cook the bacon for 5 mins until crispy. Take the bacon out and brown the beef in the bacon fat for 5 mins. Sprinkle flour over the beef, add the marinade and 500ml of water, heat up and season with salt and pepper. Put the lid on and braise in the preheated oven for 2 hrs 30 mins.

Peel the shallots and carrots. Peel and roughly chop the turnips. Peel potatoes and cut into small pieces. Halve the prunes. Add the vegetables, prunes and bacon to the casserole after approximately 1 hr 30 mins. Stir occasionally, adding extra liquid if necessary.

Apple and cider pan-fried chicken with chive mash

Serves 4

4 skinned and boned chicken breasts

salt and black pepper

2 eating apples, cored and thickly sliced

6 sage leaves, shredded

750g potatoes

1 tbsp cold-pressed rapeseed oil

25g butter

1 tsp light muscovado sugar

100ml dry cider

4 tbsp snipped fresh chives

2 tbsp double cream

Place the chicken breasts between two sheets of baking parchment and flatten with a rolling pin. Season with salt and pepper.

Peel the potatoes and cut into 2cm chunks. Cook in a pan of lightly salted boiling water for 15 mins until tender.

Heat the oil in a heavy-based frying pan over a high heat and quickly brown the chicken on both sides. Remove from the pan.

Reduce the heat and add half the butter to the pan. Toss the apple slices together with the sugar and the sage. Add to the pan and cook for 2 mins until the sugar begins to caramelize. Add the cider.

Return the chicken to the pan. Reduce the heat and simmer for 10 mins, until the chicken is cooked through and the apple slices are tender. When the potatoes are tender, drain well and add the remaining butter. Mash well. Beat in the chives and keep warm.

Remove the chicken from the pan and place on to warm serving plates with the apple slices on top. Return the pan to the stove and increase the heat. Stir in the double cream and boil rapidly until reduced slightly and pour over the chicken. Serve with the chive mash.

Stuffed pork shoulder

Serves 6

2kg boned pork shoulder

100g pitted ready-to-eat prunes, chopped

1 onion, chopped

2 tbsp cold-pressed rapeseed oil

grated zest and juice ½ lemon

75g fresh breadcrumbs

salt and black pepper

1 egg

300ml vegetable stock

Preheat the oven to 220°C/gas mark 7. Heat the oil in a frying pan and sauté the onion for 3-4 mins until softened. Tip into a mixing bowl with 75g of chopped prunes, breadcrumbs, lemon juice and zest. Mix well and season with salt and pepper. Add the egg and mix well.

Lay the pork shoulder opened out, skin-side down on a board and season with salt and pepper. Spread the stuffing over the meat. Roll the meat up and tie securely with string. Score the skin at 1cm intervals with a sharp knife, and rub all over with a little salt. Place in a large roasting pan and roast in the preheated oven for 30 mins.

Reduce the oven temperature to 160°C/gas mark 3. Roast for a further 1 hr 20 mins, until the pork is cooked The juices should run clear when the pork is pierced at its thickest part with a skewer.

Remove the pork from the tin and allow to rest while making the gravy. Spoon off the excess fat and add the remaining prunes to the pan with the stock. Bring to the boil then reduce the heat and simmer for 15 mins. Thickly slice the pork and serve with the prune gravy.

Wild mushroom stew

Serves 6

450g assorted wild mushrooms, roughly chopped if large.

50g butter

3 tbsp olive oil

3 medium shallots

750g assorted root vegetables, peeled and chopped into similar-sized chunks

200ml chicken stock

3 tbsp red wine

2 large handfuls of fresh baby spinach

salt and pepper

Put the oil and butter into a large heavy-bottomed saucepan. Heat gently. Add the shallots, increase the heat, and sweat until golden. Add the root vegetables, stirring thoroughly to ensure they are covered in the oil and butter. Cook with the lid on the pan for 5 mins.

Add half the mushrooms with the stock and wine. Bring to the boil and simmer for 10 mins. Add the remaining mushrooms, lower the heat and cook gently for a further 20 mins until the root vegetables are soft. Take the pan off the heat and add the spinach.

Let the pan rest for 5 mins before seasoning with salt and pepper.

Tarragon chicken casserole

Serves 4

400g chicken fillet

2 stems fresh tarragon, or 1 tsp dried

2 leeks

1 tin (425ml) large white beans

125g sugar snap peas

2 garlic cloves

1 tbsp oil

salt and pepper

400ml vegetable stock

150ml whipping cream

Discard the top ⅓ of each leek, wash and clean them. Cut into 1-2cm thick rings. Drain the juice off the beans, run under cold water and drain again.

Wash chicken, pat dry and cut into pieces. Wash sugar snap peas. Peel the garlic cloves and cut in half if large.

Heat oil in a pan. Add chicken and stir-fry for 3-5 mins until golden. Season with salt and pepper. Add the leek, garlic and vegetable stock and cook together for 8-10 mins. If using dried tarragon, add at this point. Add the beans and peas and cook for a further 5 mins. If using fresh tarragon, chop leaves finely. Add with cream to the stew and boil. Season casserole to taste.

"O hour, of all hours, the most bless'd upon earth,
The blessed hour of our dinners!"

Lord Lytton

Marmalade pork steaks

Serves 4

4 pork steaks

salt and black pepper

6 tbsp coarse-cut
orange marmalade

2 tbsp Worcestershire sauce

2 tbsp wholegrain mustard

Season the pork steaks with salt and
pepper. Place in a flameproof casserole dish
and place under a hot grill for 3 mins. Turn
over and cook for a further 3 mins.

Combine all the remaining ingredients.
Liberally cover one side of the pork steaks
with half the mixture. Cook for 2 mins
until beginning to turn golden. Turn over
the pork and cover with the remaining
marinade and cook for 2 mins.

Serve on warm plates with any juices
spooned over the steaks.

Roast pork belly with lentils

Serves 4

8 pork belly slices

1 onion, sliced

2 garlic cloves, crushed

1 tbsp cold-pressed rapeseed oil

2 tsp fennel seeds

salt and black pepper

400ml dry cider

150g Puy lentils

large handful fresh
parsley, coarsely chopped

Preheat the oven to 220°C/gas mark 7.
Place the pork in a roasting tin, skin side
up and roast for 20 mins. Reduce the heat
to 170°C/gas mark 3 and cook for a further
40 mins.

Heat the oil in a large saucepan over a low
heat and fry the onion and garlic for 5
mins. Add the fennel seeds and season well.
Pour in the cider and bring to the boil. Stir
in the lentils and boil for 2 mins, then
reduce the heat and simmer for 15 mins.

Remove the pork from the roasting tin and
pour off most of the fat. Add the lentils and
stir into the juice. Place the pork on top of
the lentils and cook for a further 20-25
mins, until the lentils are tender and most
of the liquid has been absorbed.

Place the pork on warm serving plates,
stir the parsley into the lentils and
serve next to the pork.

Hedgerow terrine

Serves 6

750g prepared hedgerow fruits

150ml red wine

5 tbsp golden caster sugar

8 slices day-old sour dough bread

clotted cream to serve

Place the fruit and red wine in a saucepan with 4 tbsp of golden caster sugar. Cook gently for 15 mins until the fruit is soft. Taste, adding extra sugar if it is required.

Remove the crusts from the bread. Spoon a little juice from the fruit into a non-stick 900g loaf tin. Line the base of the tin with slices of bread. Using a draining spoon, add half the fruit. Continue layering the fruit and bread, finishing with a layer of bread.

Pour the juice from the pan into the tin. Allow to cool, then chill in the refrigerator for a minimum of 8 hrs and a maximum of 24 hrs.

Carefully turn out the terrine onto a dish. Cut into slices and serve with the clotted cream.

Cobnut meringues

Serves 4

125g cobnuts

4 medium egg whites, at room temperature

250g golden caster sugar

2 tbsp vegetable oil

4 drops vanilla extract

1 tspn white wine vinegar

half a lemon

whipped cream for serving

Preheat the oven to 200°C/gas mark 6. Line two circular 20cm cake tins with foil. Grease the base and sides with the oil.

Toast the nuts in a pan, shaking occasionally to prevent burning. When cool, break up roughly.

Rub the half lemon around the insides of a bowl to remove any grease, and leave for 5 mins. Place the egg whites in the bowl and whisk until stiff. Fold in the caster sugar a little at a time. Add the vinegar, vanilla extract and nuts.

Spoon the mixture into the two cake tins. Bake for 10 mins, then turn down the heat and cook for a further 30 mins. Let the meringues cool completely before using. Fill with cream.

Steamed chocolate pudding with hedgerow fruit syrup

Serves 4

500g mixed hedgerow fruits

100g plain (70% cocoa solids) chocolate

100g butter

100g golden caster sugar

2 eggs

100g self raising flour

75g light Muscovado sugar

75ml orange juice

4 tbsp port

1 tbsp cornflour

Break the chocolate into pieces. Melt in a heatproof bowl over a pan of gently simmering water. Remove from the heat and leave to cool.

Cream the butter and sugar together until light and fluffy. Add the eggs one at a time, beating well after each addition. First fold in the flour, then the melted chocolate.

Grease a 1 litre pudding basin with butter before spooning in the chocolate cake mixture. Cover with a piece of baking parchment, then foil and tie in place. Place in a saucepan, and pour boiling water into the pan so it comes half way up the side of the basin. Cover and simmer for 1½ hrs until springy to the touch.

To make the hedgerow syrup, place the fruit and sugar in a small saucepan with the sugar and orange juice. Cook gently until the fruit is just tender. Mix 1-2 tbsp port with the cornflour to form a smooth paste, then stir in the remaining port. Add to the pan and cook, gently stirring until the juices thicken.

Turn out the chocolate pudding onto a warm serving plate. Pour the hedgerow syrup over the top and serve.

Upside down plum tart

Serves 6

For the pastry
50g blanched hazelnuts
125g plain flour
25g icing sugar
75g butter
2 egg yolks

For the topping
8-10 plums
75g butter
75g golden caster sugar
1 tsp chopped fresh rosemary

Preheat the oven to 200°C/gas mark 6.
For the pastry: place the hazelnuts in a food processor and blitz to finely chop, add the flour and icing sugar and blitz again. Add the butter cut into cubes. Process until the mixture resembles fine breadcrumbs. Add the egg yolks and mix to a soft dough, adding a little cold water if required. Cover and allow the pastry to rest for 15 mins.

Roll the pastry out on to a lightly floured work surface to a 25cm circle. Place the pastry on a baking sheet, and chill until required.

For the topping: place the remaining butter and sugar in a 23cm frying pan with an oven-proof handle. Cook over a medium heat, stirring occasionally until the mixture begins to caramelise and turn into toffee. Remove from the heat.

Cut the plums in half, discard the stones and arrange the plums cut side up in the pan. Sprinkle with the rosemary. Lift the pastry over the plums and tuck the edges down into the pan.

Bake in a preheated oven for 25-30 mins until the pastry is crisp and golden. Leave the tart in the pan for 5 mins, before turning out on a warm plate.

Blackberry omelette

Serves 2

250g blackberries
2 tbsp icing sugar
4 eggs
2 tbsp single cream
2 tbsp caster sugar
15g butter
½ tsp ground cinnamon

Mash 150g of the blackberries together with the icing sugar and push through a nylon sieve to make a blackberry coulis. Set aside.

Separate the eggs, place the eggs yolks in a bowl with the cream and 1 tbsp of the caster sugar and mix well. Mix the remaining caster sugar with the cinnamon and set aside.

Whisk the egg whites until standing in stiff peaks, then carefully fold into the yolk mixture.

Preheat a grill to high. Melt the butter in a large non-stick frying pan, pour in the omelette mixture and spread out evenly. Cook gently for 2-3 mins until the underside of the omelette is golden. Place the pan under the grill until the top is just golden.

Toss the blackberries over the top of the omelette and sprinkle with most of the cinnamon sugar. Slide out on to a warm serving plate, folding the omelette in half. Sprinkle with the remaining cinnamon sugar and drizzle over the blackberry coulis.

"There is no love sincerer than the love of food."

George Bernard Shaw, *Man and Superman*

Damson Betties

Serves 4

500g damsons
2 medium Bramley cooking apples
150g fresh breadcrumbs
85g demerara sugar
1 tsp cinnamon
2 tbsp golden caster sugar
50g chopped toasted hazelnuts
50g butter

Preheat oven to 200°C/gas mark 6.
Spread the breadcrumbs out in a thin layer on a baking sheet. Toast in the oven for 10-12 mins until crisp. Move the crumbs around during the cooking so they toast evenly. Place in a bowl and stir in the demerara sugar and cinnamon.

Cut the damsons in half, removing the stones. Place in a bowl. Peel, core and slice the apple. Toss the apples and damsons in the caster sugar.

Divide one third of the breadcrumbs equally between four individual ovenproof dishes. Layer half the fruit on top of the crumbs, top with another layer of crumbs then the rest of the fruit.

Stir the hazelnuts into the remaining crumb mixture. Melt the butter, pour over the crumbs and toss to combine well. Spread in a layer on top of the fruit. Reduce the oven temperature to 160°C/gas mark 3. Bake for 30-40 mins until the crumbs are crisp and golden. Serve with whipped cream or custard.

Apple crumble pie

Serves 4

For the pastry

250g flour

125g butter plus extra
for greasing

1 tbsp icing sugar

1 medium egg yolk

For the crumble

50g plain flour

60g butter

60g caster sugar

30g coarse oats

For the filling

750g apples

2 tbsp lemon juice

40g raisins

1 tbsp caster sugar

100g block marzipan

1 medium egg

Flour for rolling out

Preheat the oven to 200°C/gas mark 6.
For the pastry: put the flour in a bowl, add the butter and mix with the fingertips to a crumbly texture. Add icing sugar, egg yolk and 2 tbsp cold water and knead into a smooth mix. Wrap in foil and leave somewhere cold for 30 mins.

For the crumble: mix together the flour, sugar, soft butter and oats.

For the filling: peel, quarter and core apples. Cut into slices and mix with lemon juice, 1 tbsp sugar and raisins. Mix marzipan with egg.

Grease four 12cm ovenproof pie dishes. Divide pastry into four and roll out four circles 16cm across on a lightly floured sheet of baking parchment. Put one into each dish.

Divide marzipan mix equally between dishes and put apples on top. Sprinkle with crumble topping. Bake for 30-40 mins on the second lowest shelf of the pre-heated oven.

Pear, apple and blackberry compote

Serves 6

4 ripe pears
2 apples
300g blackberries
100g golden granulated sugar
6 cloves
1 cinnamon stick
2 star anise
1 vanilla pod

Place the sugar, cloves, cinnamon, star anise
and vanilla pod in a large saucepan, with
400ml of cold water. Gently bring to the
boil, stirring until the sugar has dissolved.
Simmer gently while the fruit is prepared.

Peel, core and thickly slice the apples and
pears. Add them to the simmering spiced
sugar liquid and cook for 5 mins. When the
apples and pears are tender, add the
blackberries and cook for a further 4-5 mins.
Turn off the heat and leave to cool. Discard
the spices before serving.

Cobnut and chocolate tart

Serves 8

For the pastry

330g plain flour

100g icing sugar
(plus extra for dusting)

200g chilled butter

3 eggs

pinch of salt

For the filling

200g cobnuts, roughly smashed

400g dark chocolate

250ml double cream

150ml milk

2 eggs

Preheat the oven to 180°C/gas mark 4. Lightly grease a 23cm loose-bottomed baking tin.

For the pastry: place the sugar and salt into a large bowl. Sift in the flour and stir to mix. Dice the butter, rubbing it into the flour with the tips of the fingers, and lifting the flour so that it falls through the air. Once the mixture looks like breadcrumbs, add two beaten eggs and knead to make a loose dough. Do not over-work. Put into a plastic bag and refrigerate for an hour.

Flour a surface and roll out the dough until it is 2mm in depth. Line the baking tin with the pastry, cover with baking paper and bake blind, weighting the paper with baking beans or dried peas, for 20 mins. Take the pastry from the oven, remove the paper and the beans, and brush with the third beaten egg. Bake for 2 mins, then brush more egg over the inside of the pastry case to seal it.

For the filling: lower the temperature of the oven to 130°C/gas mark ½.

Toast the nuts in a pan, shaking occasionally to prevent burning. Break the chocolate into pieces and place in a bowl.

Bring the cream and milk to the boil in a pan. Pour over the chocolate, stirring until all is blended. Whisk in the eggs.

Pour the chocolate into the pastry case and scatter the nuts over the top. Bake for 20 mins then remove from the oven. The tart will continue to set as it chills. Dust with icing sugar to serve.

Blackberry Manchester tart

For the pastry

225g plain flour

2 tbsp icing sugar

115g butter cut into cubes

For the filling

200g blackberries

250ml full-fat milk

3 egg yolks

50g golden caster sugar

2 tsp cornflour

½ tsp vanilla extract

75g blackberry jam

6 tbsp desiccated coconut

150ml double cream

Preheat the oven to 200°C/gas mark 6.
For the pastry: place the flour and icing sugar into a mixing bowl and add the butter. Rub the butter until the mixture resembles fine breadcrumbs. Add enough cold water to mix to a dough then allow to rest for 10 mins. Roll out the pastry and line a 20cm round fluted flan case or 6 individual flan cases. Chill for a minimum of 30 mins.

Line the pastry case with baking parchment and fill with baking beans. Bake for 10 mins. Remove the paper and beans. Bake for 10-12 mins until crisp and golden. Leave to cool.

For the filling: Bring the milk to the boil in a saucepan. Beat together the egg yolks, golden caster sugar, cornflour and vanilla extract until well combined. Pour in the hot milk, whisking continuously until the mixture is smooth. Return the mixture to the pan. Stirring continuously, cook until it is thick enough to coat the back of the spoon. Transfer to a clean bowl and cover with a sheet of dampened baking parchment. Set aside to cool, then chill in the fridge for 30 mins. Spread the jam over the base of the pastry case and sprinkle with half of the coconut. Place half the blackberries into the cases.

Whisk the double cream until standing in soft peaks. Fold into the chilled custard mixture until well combined. Spoon the custard and cream mixture into the pastry case in an even layer.

Top with the remaining blackberries and sprinkle with the desiccated coconut. Chill until ready to serve.

Rosehip and cardamom cake

Serves 8

200g *Rosa rugosa* rosehips

15-20 cardamom pods, according to taste

zest and juice of 2 oranges

175g golden caster sugar, plus extra for sprinkling

175g unsalted butter, at room temperature

3 large eggs

175g self raising flour, sifted

½ tsp baking powder

Top and tail the rosehips, then leave in the freezer overnight to facilitate removing the seeds. Slice the hips in half with a sharp knife and the seeds pop out of the shells.

Preheat the oven to 160°C/gas mark 3. Grease and line a 900g loaf tin with baking paper.

Using the end of a rolling pin, crack the cardamom pods open and remove the seeds from the shells. Set the seed to one side and reserve the shells.

Simmer the rosehips and cardamon shells lightly in the orange juice for 5 mins in a small pan. Turn off the heat and leave to cool. Remove the rosehips and cut into quarters.

In a mixing bowl, cream together the butter and golden caster sugar with the orange zest and cardamom seeds until fluffy. Gradually add the eggs, including a drift of flour with the last egg to prevent the mixture from curdling. Fold in the rest of the flour, with the baking powder, a little at a time. Fold half the rosehips evenly into the mixture. Spoon the mixture into the tin. Gently push down any hips above the surface.

Bake for 45 mins until a skewer pushed into the cake comes out clean. Remove from oven and scatter the remaining rosehips over the cake.

Remove the cardamom shells from the orange juice. Pour the juice, with a final sprinkle of sugar, over the top of the cake. Return to the oven for another 5 mins.

Hedgerow shortcake tart

Serves 8

300g mixture of blackberries,
raspberries and bilberries

275g self-raising flour

75g butter, softened

100g golden caster sugar

150ml milk

2 tbsp icing sugar, plus extra to dust

400ml double cream

½ tsp vanilla extract

Preheat the oven to 200°C/gas mark 6. Sift the flour
into a mixing bowl. Cut the butter into cubes and
add to the flour. Using fingertips, rub in until the
mixture resembles coarse breadcrumbs. Stir in the
caster sugar. Add enough milk to mix to a soft
dough, then roll out on a lightly floured work
surface. Place in a 23cm round loose bottom flan tin.
Prick the base with a fork and bake in the preheated
oven for 15-20 mins until golden. Allow to cool in
the tin.

Remove from the tin and place on serving plate.
Whip the cream with the icing sugar and vanilla
extract, until standing in soft peaks. Spread over the
shortcake and top with the fresh fruit.

Dust with a little more icing sugar and serve.

Pear and ginger loaf

Makes 1 loaf

4 ripe pears

3 pieces stem ginger

350g self-raising flour

3 eggs

125g butter

175g light muscovado sugar

Preheat the over to 190°C/gas mark 5. Sift the flour into a mixing bowl, making a well in the centre and add the eggs. Melt the butter and sugar together in a saucepan. Start to beat the eggs into the flour with a wooden spoon and gradually adding the butter and sugar mixture until well combined.

Peel and core the pears. Dice half the pears and coarsely grate the other half. Finely chop the ginger. Beat the pear and ginger into the flour mixture. Transfer to the prepared tin.

Bake in the preheated oven for 1 hr until risen and golden and a skewer inserted into the centre comes out clean. Allow to stand in the tin for 10 mins before transferring to a wire rack to cool completely.

Serve sliced, lightly buttered.

Apple and almond cake

Serves 8

2 small apples

100g ground almonds plus extra
for tin

180g butter plus extra
for greasing

140g caster sugar

1 tsp vanilla extract

3 medium eggs

150g self raising flour

50ml milk

Icing sugar for sprinkling

Preheat the over to 200°C/gas mark 6.
Beat the butter, sugar and vanilla extract
together until creamy. Mix the eggs in one
by one, then the almonds. Add the flour
and milk and beat again.

Grease a 22cm spring-clip round cake tin,
scatter the base with ground almonds, put
in the cake mixture and level the top.

Cut the apples into slices and arrange on
the cake mixture in a fan pattern. Bake the
cake on the second lowest shelf of the
preheated oven for 45 mins. If need be,
cover with foil for the last 10 mins to stop
the top over browning. Turn out, and leave
the finished cake to cool on a wire tray.

Sprinkle with icing sugar and serve with
whipped cream.

"Winter is the time for comfort, for good food and warmth, for the touch of a friendly hand and for a talk beside the fire: it is the time for home."

Edith Sitwell

WINTER

THE GROUND OUTSIDE may be cloaked in frost, but winter is far from a subdued time in the kitchen. Colour comes in many forms and shades. Sweet, juicy Clementines are coveted for their balance of tart and sweetness. They can be used to decorate cakes, flavour puddings, or fill stockings. Pomegranate is used in both sweet and savoury dishes at this time of year, their magenta arils shining jewel-like.

Vegetables are a staple of the winter kitchen, bulking out warming soups and stews. The slow cooking process of roasting caramelises the natural sugars of root vegetables, releasing their sweet flavours. Cabbage comes in many forms – round, oblong and even pointy – and a variety of colours from subtle white to bold dark green. All are highly nutritious, packed with vitamins A, K and C and iron.

Such strong flavours need meat pairings that are equally robust. Venison, in season now, has an intense gamey flavour. Farmed meat is more tender, whereas the tougher wild meat is delicious slow-cooked in red wine. Pheasant is also readily available now, but the bird that says winter like no other is the turkey. On butchers' and supermarket shelves other meats make way for this most majestic of birds.

Christmas brings a hive of activity. Mince pies are filled with homemade mincemeat spiced with the quintessential flavours of the festivities, cinnamon, nutmeg and cloves. Rich, dark fruit cakes are baked ready to take their place at the centre of the table. This is the time for making edible gifts, filled with love and flavour.

Potato and Savoy cabbage soup

Serves 4

250g Savoy cabbage
8 rashers of smoked streaky bacon
1 tbsp cold-pressed rapeseed oil
1 leek
1 stick celery
600g King Edward potatoes
1.25 litre chicken stock
salt and pepper

Chop the bacon into thin strips. Heat the oil in a large saucepan and fry the bacon pieces until golden and crisp. Remove with a slotted spoon and set to one side.

Finely slice the leek and celery and add to pan. Stir to coat in the oil then cook for 5-10 mins over a gentle heat until softened.

Peel and dice the potatoes and add to the pan, stirring to combine. Cook gently for 2-3 mins. Add the stock and bring to the boil, then reduce to a simmer and cook, covered, for 15 mins. Blend until smooth, seasoning to taste.

Finely shred the cabbage and add to the soup. Cook for a further 10 mins, until just tender. Serve with the bacon pieces sprinkled over the top.

Gateshead floddies

4 rashers streaky bacon, chopped

600g potatoes, peeled and coarsely grated

1 small onion, coarsely grated

25g self-raising flour

salt and black pepper

2 eggs

cold-pressed rapeseed oil for frying

Dry fry the bacon until crisp, then remove from the pan and set to one side.

Place the potatoes in a sieve and squeeze out as much liquid as possible. Pat dry with kitchen paper and place in a large mixing bowl. Add the grated onions to the potatoes, along with the cooled bacon. Stir in the flour, salt and pepper, add the egg and mix well.

Heat the oil in a large frying pan over a medium heat. Cook large spoonfuls of the mixture for 3-4 mins on each side, until golden and crisp.

Remove and keep warm while the remaining mixture is cooked, using more oil as necessary.

Shropshire pea soup

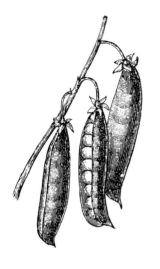

Serves 4

500g peas
1 onion, finely chopped
25g butter
large sprig mint, plus mint leaves to garnish
900ml vegetable stock
salt and pepper
100ml double cream, plus extra to serve

Melt the butter in a large saucepan and add the onion. Cook over a low heat for 10 mins, stirring occasionally, until the onion softens and begins to brown.

Remove the leaves from the mint sprig and add to the pan with the peas and stock. Bring to a boil, then reduce the heat. Simmer gently for 15 mins until the peas are tender. Blitz in a food processor until smooth.

Season to taste then stir in the double cream, reheating without boiling. Serve garnished with the mint leaves and a swirl of extra cream.

Winter potato salad

800g small salad potatoes

3 tbsp cider wine vinegar

4 tbsp cold-pressed rapeseed oil

1 tsp wholegrain mustard

½ tsp caster sugar

2 tbsp chopped gherkins

2 tsp capers

salt and black pepper

4 tbsp chopped fresh chives

260g hot smoked trout

Cut the potatoes in half and cook in a large pan of lightly salted boiling water until tender. Drain thoroughly and tip into a serving bowl.

Whisk the vinegar, oil, mustard and sugar together. Add the gherkins and capers then season to taste. Pour the dressing over the warm potatoes. Sprinkle over the chives and gently stir to mix.

Flake the trout into bite-sized pieces and arrange on top of the potatoes. Serve immediately.

"What I can say is that, if a man really likes potatoes, he must be a pretty decent sort of fellow."

A A Milne, *Lunch*

Arbroath smokies

Serves 6

400g smoked haddock

2 medium eggs

50g butter plus extra to grease the ramekins

20g flour

250ml milk

70g cheddar cheese

salt and pepper

Preheat the oven to 175°C/gas mark 4. Hard boil the eggs then plunge into cold water and leave to cool.

Melt 30g butter in a pan and sprinkle with flour, cooking for 1 min. Stir in the milk gradually, heat up and simmer over a low heat for 5 mins, continuing to stir. Grate the cheese and add one spoonful to the sauce at a time so it melts. Season with salt and pepper, and leave to cool.

Grease six ramekins. Remove the fish skin and bones and cut into small pieces. Shell the eggs and chop them up.

Mix the fish and eggs with the sauce and fill the ramekins. Sprinkle with the remaining cheese. Bake in the preheated oven for 20 mins.

Serve with warm buttered toast.

English breakfast hash

Serves 2

500g new potatoes
1 red onion
2 pork sausages
20g butter
1 tbsp cold-pressed rapeseed oil
1 tsp chopped fresh thyme
4 rashers streaky smoked bacon
2 ripe tomatoes, roughly chopped
salt and black pepper
2 large eggs

Cut the potatoes into small cubes. Blanch for 5 mins in lightly salted boiling water. Peel and chop the onion. Remove the sausage meat from the skin and break into pieces. Cook in a heavy-based frying pan for 5 mins. Break it up as it cooks so there are small browned pieces of sausage meat. Remove from the pan.

Add the butter and oil to the pan. Stir in the onion and thyme and cook for 3 mins. Add the potatoes. Stir and press down frequently for 5-10 mins until the potato begins to crisp and turn golden.

Snip the bacon into pieces and add to the pan. Return the sausage meat to the pan with the chopped tomatoes. Season with salt and pepper and cook for 5-10 mins, until the tomato softens and the sausage is piping hot. Make 2 holes in the potato mixture and drop in the eggs.

Cover and cook for 3 mins until the whites have set and the yolks are hot. Serve immediately.

Pot roast pheasant

Serves 4

2 pheasant
500ml chicken stock
100ml cold water
100g pearl barley
salt and pepper
30g butter
2 tbsp cold-pressed rapeseed oil
8 shallots
350g carrots
300g parsnips
200g turnips
2 celery stalks
4 sprigs of thyme
2 bay leaves
8 juniper berries
250ml sweet sherry

Preheat the oven to 220°C/gas mark 7. Pour 300ml of the chicken stock into a saucepan with 100ml cold water and the pearl barley. Bring to the boil and stir in ½ tsp of salt. Reduce the heat to a simmer and cover. Cook for 30 mins until just tender.

Season the pheasants inside and out. Melt the butter with the oil in a large ovenproof casserole and brown the meat all over. Remove the birds from the pan and reduce the heat. Add the shallots and cook until golden.

Chop the carrots, parsnips and turnips into small bite-sized pieces. Add to the shallots with the thyme. Cook, stirring occasionally, until the vegetables start to brown. Add the remaining ingredients, along with the cooked pearl barley and chicken stock. Season to taste.

Stir to mix, then place the pheasants on top. Bring to the boil. Cover and cook in the oven for 20 mins. Remove the lid and cook for a further 10 mins.

Remove from the oven and leave to rest in a warm place for 10 mins before carving. Serve with the vegetables and pearl barley.

Beef and anchovy casserole

Serves 4

650g braising steak

3 anchovies

2 tbsp cold-pressed rapeseed oil

1 large onion, roughly chopped

75g diced bacon

2 cloves garlic

350g carrots

500g leeks

2 bay leaves

300g large tomatoes

3 tbsp plain flour

600ml beef stock

salt and pepper

100ml single cream

Cut the beef into large chunks. Heat half the oil in a shallow, heavy-based pan and fry the meat in batches, browning all sides. Remove the meat with a draining spoon and set aside.

Finely chop the garlic and anchovies. Peel and chop the carrots and onions. Slice and wash the leeks. Cut the tomatoes in half.

Add the remaining oil to the pan. Cook the onion and bacon over a moderate heat until the onion starts to soften and the bacon begins to crisp. Stir the garlic and anchovies into the pan. Add the carrots and leeks. Continue cooking till the leeks are lightly browned, then add the bay leaves and the tomatoes.

Return the meat to the pan with any juices. Stir in the flour and cook for 2 mins. Pour in the beef stock and season to taste. Bring to the boil, then lower the heat and cover. Leave to simmer gently for 1½ hrs until the meat is tender.

Stir the cream into the casserole just before serving.

"But we hae meat, and we can eat,
And sae the Lord be thankit."

Robert Burns, 'The Selkirk Grace'

Celeriac and lamb hotpot

Serves 6

1 small celeriac

800g stewing lamb

1 large onion, peeled and sliced

2 carrots, peeled and chopped

2 tbsp rapeseed oil

2 tbsp plain flour

2 tbsp Worcestershire sauce

400ml lamb or beef stock

2 large potatoes

25g butter

Preheat the oven to 160°C/gas mark 3. Peel and dice the celeriac. Heat 1 tbsp of the oil in a large frying pan and brown the lamb in batches over a high heat. Remove each batch to a plate.

Add the remaining oil to the pan. Add the onion and cook until softened. Add the carrots and celeriac. Cook, while stirring, until the vegetables start to brown.

Return the lamb and any juices to the pan and stir to mix. Sprinkle the flour in, continuing to stir, and cook for 1 min. Add the Worcestershire sauce and the stock a little at a time, stirring well between each addition. When all the stock has been added, transfer the mixture to a casserole dish.

Peel and thinly slice the potatoes and layer over the top of the lamb and vegetables to cover. Dot the top with butter and cover before cooking in the oven for 1 hour. Remove the lid and continue to cook for a further 45 mins until the top is golden.

Pheasant and apple casserole

Serves 4

4 pheasant breasts
salt and black pepper
1 onion, chopped
1 clove garlic, chopped
2 tbsp rapeseed oil
100g smoked bacon lardons
2 tbsp plain flour
150ml dry white wine
350ml chicken stock
2 Granny Smith apples
1 large sprig thyme
2 bay leaves

Season the pheasant. Heat the oil in a large saucepan and brown the meat. Remove and set to one side. Add the onion and bacon to the pan. Cook until the onion has softened, then add the garlic.

Sprinkle over the flour and stir, cooking for 1 min. Add the wine and stock a little at a time, stirring well between each addition to ensure no lumps form.

Peel and thickly slice the apples. Add to the pan with the thyme and bay leaves. Return the pheasant to the pan and bring to the boil. Reduce the heat and simmer gently for 20 mins.

Rolled and stuffed turkey breast and gravy

Serves 8

2kg skinless boneless
turkey breast

For the stuffing

50g dried cranberries

25g pecans

1 onion

zest 1 orange

75g sourdough breadcrumbs

500g good quality pork
sausagemeat

salt and pepper

For the topping

4 rashers thin cut smoked
streaky bacon

25g pecans

15g dried cranberries

50g coarse sourdough
breadcrumbs

2 tbsp cranberry jelly

For the gravy

1 litre poultry stock

2 tbsp plain flour

150ml port

2 tbsp cranberry jelly

Preheat the oven to 200°C/
gas mark 6.

For the stuffing: Place roughly
chopped cranberries and pecans in a
mixing bowl. Peel and finely chop the
onion. Add to the bowl with the finely
grated zest of the orange. Add the
breadcrumbs and sausagemeat. Season
with salt and pepper, mixing until
well combined.

For the turkey: Place the turkey on a
large sheet of cling film and slit it
lengthways, horizontally. Cut almost
but not all the way through so that it
remains joined on one side. Open it
out and cover with another sheet of
cling film. Flatten out using a rolling
pin until the meat is an even
thickness.

Spread about two-thirds of the
stuffing mix down the length of the
turkey breast. Roll the meat up and
secure with string. Place on a rack over
a large roasting tin. Pour 400ml
boiling water into the roasting tin.
Cover with a tent of foil and pinch the
edges to the tin to seal. Cook in the
preheated oven for 20 mins then
reduce the temperature to 150°C/
gas mark 2. Cook for a further 2 hrs.

For the topping: Finely chop the
bacon and dry fry until crisp. Chop
the pecans and cranberries and add to

the pan with the breadcrumbs. Cook,
stirring, until the bread is lightly
toasted in places. Set to one side.

Roll the remaining stuffing into eight
balls and place in a small lightly oiled
baking tin. Remove the turkey from
the oven and transfer to a serving
plate. Set to one side to rest. Increase
the oven temperature to 190°C/
gas mark 5 and place the stuffing balls
in the oven to cook for 25 mins.

To make the gravy, pour the juices
from the roasting tin into a bowl.
Spoon off the fat that floats to the
surface. Place the roasting tin on a
high heat, add flour and stir to scrape
sediment from the tin. Cook for 1
min. Pour in the port and stir well.
Add the stock, bring to boil and
simmer for 5 mins. Add the turkey
juices, bring back to the boil and cook
for a further 3 mins. Add cranberry
jelly and stir until dissolved. Strain
into a serving jug.

Spread the top of the turkey with the
cranberry jelly. Sprinkle and press the
topping over the turkey and serve with
the stuffing balls alongside.

Venison with red wine and juniper berries

Serves 4

750g casserole venison

100ml red wine

6 juniper berries

250g baby onions, peeled and chopped

2 cloves garlic, peeled and chopped

2 tbsp plain flour

salt and black pepper

1 tsp mustard powder

cold-pressed rapeseed oil for frying

300ml beef stock

3 allspice berries

2 tbsp redcurrant jelly

100g chestnuts

100g button mushrooms

Preheat the oven to 150°C/gas mark 2. Cut the venison into chunks and place in a resealable plastic bag with the flour. Season with salt and pepper and add the mustard powder. Shake well to coat venison pieces.

Heat 1 tbsp of the oil in a heavy-based frying pan and cook the onions until they begin to colour. Transfer to an oven-proof casserole dish. Fry the venison in batches over a high heat until browned on all sides, adding more oil as required. Transfer to the casserole dish and reduce the heat under the frying pan. Add the garlic and the wine, scraping up all the juices and crispy bits from the pan. Add the stock and bring to the boil then pour over the meat and onions in the dish.

Crush the juniper berries and allspice in a pestle and mortar, and add to the casserole along with the redcurrant jelly. Cover and cook for 1 hour, then stir in the chestnuts and mushrooms. Cover again and cook for up to 1½ hrs until the meat is very tender. Check the seasoning and serve immediately.

Pan-fried fish with cabbage and peas

Serves 4

4 x 150g skin on hake fillets
1 Savoy cabbage
200g peas
4 rashers smoked streaky bacon
1 onion
1 large carrot
2 sticks celery
3 tbsp cold-pressed rapeseed oil
1 lemon
small bunch thyme
100ml dry white wine
200ml chicken stock
200g butter beans
3 tbsp plain flour
salt and pepper

Roughly chop the bacon. Peel and finely chop the onion and carrots, and slice the celery. Shred the cabbage, discarding the tough outer leaves and core.

Heat 1 tbsp of oil in a large pan. Add the bacon and cook until turning golden and crisp. Add the onion, and cook for 4-5 mins until softened. Then add the carrot and celery, cooking for a further 5 mins. Add the cabbage to the pan, stirring well to mix.

Finely grate the zest from the lemon and squeeze the juice. With a small piece of cook's string, tie the thyme into a small bunch. Add the zest, juice, thyme, wine and chicken stock to the pan and bring to the boil. Stir, then reduce the heat to a gentle simmer and season to taste.

Cover and cook over a gentle heat for 6-8 mins before adding the beans and peas. Cook for a further 3 mins. Discard the thyme.

Meanwhile, season the flour and dust the fish fillets to coat. Heat the remaining oil in a frying pan. Cook the fish, skin side down for 3-4 mins until the skin is crisp and golden. Turn over and cook for a further 2-3 mins until the fish is cooked through.

Serve the cabbage mixture with the fish on top.

Cranberry and Stilton stuffed fillet of beef

1kg piece fillet of beef

40g dried cranberries

75g Stilton

1 shallot

2 cloves garlic

85g chestnut mushrooms

30g butter

1 tbsp rapeseed oil

50g fresh white breadcrumbs

15g chopped parsley

75ml port

100ml beef stock

2 tbsp redcurrant jelly

1 tsp cornflour

Preheat the oven to 400°C/gas mark 6. Cut a slit lengthways along the beef, cutting almost but not all the way through the fillet and open out to form a pocket. Season well.

Chop the cranberries. Finely chop the shallot and garlic, and coarsely chop the mushrooms.

Heat the butter and oil in a small frying pan and add the shallots, cooking for 2 mins. Stir in the garlic and mushrooms and sauté for a further 5 mins. Remove from the heat and stir in the breadcrumbs, cranberries and parsley. Crumble in the Stilton and toss to combine. Spread the breadcrumb mixture into the beef pocket.

Tie the meat with string to enclose the stuffing. If the beef fillet is thinner at one end, fold the meat back on itself as it is tied. This ensures it is the same thickness all along the joint.

Place the joint in a roasting tin. Cook uncovered in the oven for 50 mins for rare, 1 hour for medium rare and 1 hr 10 mins for well done. Transfer to a chopping board, covering loosely with foil. Allow to rest for 15 mins while preparing the sauce.

Place the roasting tin back on the hob and add the port to the pan, stirring well and scraping the base of the pan to dislodge any sediment. Add the stock and bring to the boil for 4 mins to reduce the liquid slightly. Stir in the redcurrant jelly. Mix the cornflour with a little water and stir in. Cook until the sauce just thickens then strain into a jug. Cut the beef into thick slices and serve.

Chicken and mushroom casserole with tarragon bread

For the casserole

4 chicken joints

225g mushrooms, sliced

1 onion, peeled and sliced

1 tbsp cold-pressed rapeseed oil

25g butter

2 tbsp plain flour

200ml chicken stock

150ml milk

6 tbsp double cream

3 sprigs fresh tarragon

salt and black pepper

For the bread

1 small loaf

50g butter

4 sprigs fresh tarragon

Preheat the oven to 180°C/gas mark 4.

For the casserole: Heat the oil in a heavy-based frying pan. Add the chicken joints and brown on all sides. Transfer to an ovenproof casserole.

Add the onions to the frying pan and cook over a low heat for 5 mins, until they begin to soften. Add the butter and mushrooms and cook for a further 5 mins. Sprinkle the flour into the pan and cook for 1 min, stirring frequently. Gradually add the stock then the milk. Bring to a boil then pour over the chicken. Cover and cook in the oven for 45 mins.

Chop the tarragon and stir in to the double cream. Season to taste. Pour over the chicken and cook uncovered for 15 mins.

For the bread: Cut the loaf into 2cm thick slices. Beat the butter until softened, then chop the tarragon and beat into the butter. Spread each slice of bread with butter then sandwich the slices back together to reform the loaf. Wrap in foil. Bake with the chicken for 15 mins then serve alongside.

White chocolate trifle with gingerbread

Serves 8

For the gingerbread

200g self-raising flour

100g light muscovado sugar

½ tsp bicarbonate of soda

1½ tsp ground ginger

100g butter

125ml whole milk

3 tbsp black treacle

2 eggs

For the trifle

300g white chocolate

350g mascarpone

400ml double cream

zest of 1 large orange

Preheat the oven to 160°C/gas mark 3.
For the gingerbread: Grease and line a 20cm square tin. Mix the dry ingredients in a large bowl. Melt the butter and add to the bowl, with the milk and treacle. Stir well until blended. Leave to cool then beat in the eggs. Add this mixture to the dried ingredients, beating until smooth.

Pour into the prepared tin. Bake in the preheated oven for 35 mins until cooked through and springy to the touch. Cool in the tin before turning out and cutting into cubes.

For the trifle: Chop the chocolate into small pieces and put in a bowl with the mascarpone. Place over a pan of gently simmering water. Cook without stirring until the chocolate has melted. Remove from the heat and cool for 5 mins, then stir gently.

Whip the cream until it stands in soft peaks and fold into the chocolate mixture. Scatter a third of the gingerbread in the base of the trifle bowl. Top with a third of the white chocolate mixture. Repeat layers, finishing with the white chocolate. Sprinkle with the orange zest.

Orange self-saucing pudding

Serves 4

finely grated zest and
juice of 1 orange
60g butter, softened,
plus extra for greasing
75g golden caster sugar
2 medium eggs
1 tbsp thin-shred orange
marmalade
40g plain flour
175ml milk

Preheat the oven to 180°C/gas mark 4. Butter four ovenproof cups and set to one side. Beat the butter, orange zest and sugar together until they are light and creamy.

Separate the eggs. Beat the egg yolks with the marmalade. Add the orange juice and beat again before adding the flour and mixing well. Stir into the creamed butter and sugar mixture. Beat in the milk and mix well.

Whisk the egg whites until they form stiff peaks, and fold into the orange mixture. Divide between the greased cups. Place the cups in a roasting tin and add boiling water to come half way up their sides.

Bake in the preheated oven for 25 mins until the sponge is just set. Serve immediately.

Ginger pudding

Serves 8

20g fresh ginger

175g soft butter

175g light muscovado sugar

peel from ½ lemon

2 tsp and 1 tbsp ginger syrup
(from a jar of stem ginger in syrup)

4 medium eggs

175g self-raising flour

3 medium egg yolks

75g sugar

seeds scraped from half a vanilla pod

2 tsp cornflour

250g double cream

250ml milk

4 pieces stem ginger

2 tbsp golden syrup

Peel and grate the fresh ginger. Beat the butter, muscovado sugar, lemon peel and 2 tsp ginger syrup with an electric hand whisk for 5 mins.

Add the eggs one by one. Sift in the self-raising flour and grated ginger and stir in. Grease a 1.25 litre heat-resistant pudding bowl, fill it with the mixture and smooth over the top. Cover the basin with baking parchment then foil. Stand in a pan and fill halfway up with water. Cover the pan and simmer over a low heat for 45 mins.

Mix the egg yolks, sugar, vanilla seeds and cornflour together in a pan. Add the double cream and milk. Bring to the boil on a low heat, stirring constantly and leave to cool a little.

Cut the stem ginger into small pieces and stir together with 1 tbsp of ginger syrup and 2 tbsp golden syrup.

Take the pudding basin out of the pan and leave it to cool for approximately 15 mins. Upturn onto a plate or platter and wait until the pudding slides out. Remove the basin. Pour the syrup and ginger pieces over the pudding. Serve with custard.

Double chocolate orange meringue cake

Serves 8

100g dark chocolate
100g white chocolate
3 mandarins
6 egg whites
300g caster sugar
1 tsp cocoa
1 tbsp orange-flavoured liqueur
1 tbsp golden syrup
15g butter

Preheat the oven to 140°C/gas mark 2. Line two baking trays with parchment paper, marking a 20cm circle on one and a 18cm one on the other.

Place the egg whites in a large, spotlessly clean mixing bowl and whisk until stiff peaks form. Whisk in the caster sugar a spoonful at a time until the mixture is thick and glossy.

Grate 50g of the dark chocolate. Very gently fold the grated chocolate through the meringue to create a rippled effect. Spoon the mixture evenly over the two circles, and swirl it around the edges. Place the cocoa in a sieve and gently dust over the meringues. Bake in the preheated oven for 1 hr 30 mins. Turn the oven off and open the door slightly. Leave the meringues in the oven until completely cooled.

Peel and segment the mandarins. Place in a small bowl and sprinkle the orange liqueur over the segments. Set aside.

Wrap a rolling pin in parchment paper and place on a tray lined with parchment paper. Melt the remaining dark chocolate in a heatproof bowl set over a pan of gently simmering water. Take a large spoonful of the chocolate and drizzle it quickly back and forth over the rolling pin to make chocolate curls. Repeat this two or three times and leave in a cool place to set. Add the golden syrup, butter and 1 tbsp of water to the remaining chocolate in the bowl and stir until smooth and glossy.

Chop the white chocolate into small pieces. Place in a heatproof bowl with 100ml cream, over a pan of simmering water. Cook without stirring until the chocolate has melted. Remove from the heat and stir gently until just combined. Allow to cool completely. Whip the remaining cream until it forms soft peaks, then fold in the white chocolate mixture.

Place one of the meringue discs on a serving plate and top with half the white chocolate cream. Scatter two-thirds of the mandarin segments over the cream and drizzle with juice from the bowl. Top with the second meringue and the remaining cream and mandarin segments. Spoon over the dark chocolate sauce and scatter the chocolate curls.

White chocolate and clementine cheesecake with pomegranate seeds

Serves 8

300g white chocolate

6 clementines

250g gingernut biscuits

75g butter

750g full-fat cream cheese

100g golden caster sugar

300ml double cream

seeds of 1 pomegranate

Place the gingernut biscuits in a bag and crush to fine crumbs. Melt the butter in a saucepan and add the biscuit crumbs. Mix thoroughly then press into the base of a 23cm loose-bottom cake tin. Chill while making the filling.

Beat the cream cheese and caster sugar together. Whip the cream until just holding its shape and fold into the cheese mixture. Grate the zest and squeeze the juice from two of the clementines and fold in. Melt the chocolate in a bowl over a pan of hot water, then fold into the cheese mixture. Pour into the cake tin and chill until set.

When the cheesecake is set, carefully remove from the tin and transfer to a serving plate. Peel and slice the remaining clementines. Arrange with the pomegranate seeds over the top of the cheesecake and serve.

Gingerbread apple crumble

Serves 4

100g gingerbread (see page 173)

65g cold butter

1 tbsp flour

25g muscovado sugar

800g apples

juice of 1 lemon

25g whole ginger

100g raisins

pinch of ground cinnamon

Preheat the oven to 175°C/gas mark 2. Crumble up the gingerbread into little bits. Cut the butter into flecks and mix with the flour, sugar and gingerbread crumbs. Peel the apples, halve and de-core. Cut into small pieces and sprinkle with lemon juice. Peel the ginger and chop up small. Wash the raisins and drain well.

Heat up 15g butter in a pan and cook the apples, ginger, raisins and cinnamon for 2 mins. Put the apple mix in an ovenproof dish and cover with the gingerbread crumble mix. Bake in the preheated oven for 20 mins. Serve warm.

Cinnamon wreath

Serves 12

400g strong bread flour

7g sachet easy-blend yeast

3 tbsp golden caster sugar

1¼ tsp salt

25g butter

4 tbsp milk

175-250ml warm water

2 tsp ground cinnamon

250g home-made mincemeat
(see page 188)

50g icing sugar

cold water

Preheat the oven to 200°C/gas mark 6.
Place the flour into a mixing bowl and stir in the yeast, sugar
and salt. Rub in the butter. Add the milk and enough water to
mix to a soft dough.

Turn the dough out on to a lightly floured surface and knead
well for 5 mins, until smooth and elastic. Place in a lightly
oiled bowl, turning to coat the dough in the oil. Cover and
leave in a warm place to rise for 1 hour or until doubled in size.

Turn out onto a lightly floured surface, roll or press out to
form a 40 x 20cm rectangle. Place the rectangle so that the
long edge is at the front.

Stir the cinnamon into the mincemeat and spread evenly over
the dough leaving a 2cm line of dough at the far end clear of
the filling. Dampen the clean edges of the dough with a little
water and starting with the long end nearest, roll up the dough
into a tight log.

Cut into 2cm thick slices and place in a circle overlapping on a
lightly greased baking sheet. Cover loosely with oiled cling
film and leave in a warm place for 30 mins.

Uncover and bake in the preheated oven for 15-20 mins. Allow
to cool for 5 mins then carefully transfer to a wire rack to cool
completely. Mix the icing sugar with enough cold water to
form a smooth icing and drizzle back and forth over the ring to
decorate. Let the icing to set before serving.

White chocolate and cranberry slice

Serves 8

For the pastry

175g plain flour

40g ground almonds

100g butter

2 tbsp golden

caster sugar

1 egg yolk

1-2tbsp cold water

For the filling

200g white chocolate

200g cranberries

3 tbsp golden

caster sugar

grated zest and juice

½ orange

300ml double cream

Sift the flour into a mixing bowl and stir in the ground almonds. Cut the butter into cubes and rub in until the mixture resembles fine breadcrumbs. Stir in the caster sugar. Add the egg yolk and enough cold water to mix to a soft dough. Roll out and line a 35 x 12cm oblong flan tin. Chill for 30 mins. Line with baking parchment and fill with baking beans. Bake for 10 mins in a preheated oven at 200°C/gas mark 6. Remove the lining paper and beans, and bake for a further 10 mins until crisp and golden.

Place the cranberries in the saucepan with the sugar, orange zest and juice. Cook gently over a low heat until the cranberries start to soften and pop. Using a draining spoon, lift out half the cranberries and set aside. Continue to cook the remaining cranberries for a further 5 mins until very soft, then cool. Break the chocolate into pieces. Place in a heatproof bowl over a pan of simmering water, stirring until melted. Remove from pan. Whip the cream until it just holds its shape. Quickly fold in the melted chocolate.

Remove the pastry case from the tin and place on a serving dish. Spread the cranberries from the saucepan over the base of the case. Cover with the white chocolate mixture. Scatter the reserved cranberries over the top. Chill until it is time to serve.

Salted caramel chocolates

Makes 36

200ml double cream

100ml water

400g light muscovado

3 tbsp golden syrup

50g butter

¼ tsp cream of tartar

1 tsp vanilla extract

¼ tsp sea salt, plus extra to decorate

450g milk or plain chocolate

Grease and line a 18cm square cake tin with baking parchment. Fill the sink with about 10cm of cold water. Place the cream, water, sugar, golden syrup, butter, cream of tartar and salt into a large saucepan and heat gently, stirring constantly until the butter has melted and the sugar has dissolved. Place a sugar thermometer in the pan and increase the heat slowly until the mixture comes to a rolling boil (boiling rapidly with lots of bubbling) and the temperature reaches 125°C on the thermometer. As soon as the correct temperature is reached, plunge the base of the pan into the sink of cold water for a few seconds to stop it cooking further.

Remove the bowl from the sink, stir the vanilla essence into the caramel and pour the mixture into the prepared tin. Do not scrape the pan out, this will cause the mixture to turn to fudge. Allow to cool.

When the mixture is almost set, cut into pieces with an oiled knife. Chop the chocolate into pieces and melt 300g in a heatproof bowl over a pan of gently simmering water. Remove from the heat and stir in the remaining chocolate. Dip the caramels in the chocolate, allowing the excess chocolate to drip back into the bowl. Place on a sheet of baking parchment. Sprinkle with a little extra salt and allow the chocolate to set. Store in an airtight container in a cool, dry place.

Cinnamon mincemeat tart

Serve 12

For the mincemeat

250g raisins

250g currants

250g sultanas

200g candied orange and lemon peel

1 unwaxed orange

1 unwaxed lemon

400g apples

125g cold butter, cut into cubes

100g flaked almonds

¼ tsp ground nutmeg

1 tsp ground cinnamon

¼ tsp cardamom

¼ tsp ground cloves

200g brown sugar

150ml brandy

For the pastry

225g cold butter, plus extra to grease the dish

350g flour

100g caster sugar

¼ tsp ground cinnamon

salt

1 medium egg yolk

3 tbsp milk

To make the mincemeat: rinse the raisins, currants and sultanas in cold water, drain and dry off. Chop the candied orange and lemon peel. Wash the fresh orange and lemon in hot water, dry and grate off zest slivers. Halve and squeeze the citrus fruits. Peel the apples, de-core and dice the flesh. Dice the cold butter. Mix together these prepared ingredients with the almonds, nutmeg, cinnamon, cardamom, cloves and brown sugar. Cover the mixture and leave somewhere cold overnight to blend.

Preheat the oven to 125°C/lowest gas mark setting. Put the mixture in an ovenproof dish and lightly cover with foil. Bake for 3 hrs. Stir occasionally.

Take the mincemeat out, let it cool and stir in the brandy. Cover and leave to steep.

Preheat the oven to 200°C/gas mark 6.
To make the pastry: dice the butter. Mix in the flour, caster sugar, cinnamon and a pinch of salt. Grease a 21 x 28.5cm oblong baking tin. Roll out two thirds of the pastry on a floured surface into a 25 x 32cm oblong and line the tin. Spoon the mincemeat onto the pastry and spread it out. Roll out the remaining pastry, cut into strips and criss-cross in diamonds over the mincemeat. Beat the egg yolk and milk and lightly brush the pastry strips.

Bake in the preheated oven for 30 mins. Remove from oven, leave to cool and lift out of the tin.

Jewelled fruit cake

Makes around 16 slices

300g dried apricots

200g glacé cherries

200g candied orange slices

2 tsp loose black tea

6 tbsp brandy

1 tsp fine cut marmalade

150g sultanas

150g currants

2 unwaxed lemons

200g soft butter

250g muscovado sugar

4 medium eggs

200g flour

1 tsp cinnamon

¼ tsp ground cloves

¼ tsp ground nutmeg

½ tsp ground ginger

50g shelled almonds

Fat and flour for the tin

Chop the apricots, cherries and oranges coarsely but keep a few whole orange slices and cherries to decorate the cake. Pour 300ml boiling hot water on to the tea leaves and leave to draw for 3 mins. Pour the tea through a strainer. Mix together 200ml tea, 3 tbsp brandy, marmalade, sultanas, currants, apricots, chopped cherries and orange slices. Cover and leave to soak overnight.

Keep the remaining tea covered for later. Remove the lemon peel in very thin strips with a zester, and chop roughly. Beat the butter and 200g sugar together with the whisk tool of a hand mixer until creamy. Add the eggs one by one and whip again. Mix the flour, cinnamon, cloves, nutmeg and ginger. Add a tablespoonful at a time to the sugar/butter/eggs mix. Add the soaked fruit and lemon peel and fold them into the mixture.

Grease and flour a 20cm springform cake tin. Add the mixture to the tin, filling to the brim, and bake in a preheated oven (160°C/gas 3) for 1 hr 30 mins. Turn the temperature down (140°C/gas 1) and bake for a further 1 hr 30 mins. Boil the remaining tea and 50g sugar. Add 3 tbsp brandy. Take the cake out of the oven. Pierce the cake all over with a wooden skewer and brush it with the brandy/tea syrup. Leave the cake to cool, but continue brushing with syrup until none remains. Decorate the cake with the oranges, cherries and almonds.

INDEX

INDEX